WHEN DOES LIFE BEGIN?

Other Books by
John Ankerberg and John Weldon

The Case for Jesus the Messiah: Incredible Prophecies that Prove God Exists, (Chattanooga: Ankerberg Theological Research Institute, 1989).

Astrology: Do the Heavens Rule Our Destiny? (Eugene, OR: Harvest House, 1989).

Christianity and the Secret Teachings of the Masonic Lodge: What Goes on Behind Closed Doors, (Chattanooga: Ankerberg Theological Research Institute, 1989).

The Secret Teachings of the Masonic Lodge: A Christian Appraisal, (Chicago, IL: Moody Press, 1990).

The Facts on Astrology, (Eugene, OR: Harvest House, 1989).

The Facts on the Jehovah's Witnesses, (Eugene, OR: Harvest House, 1989).

The Facts on the New Age Movement, (Eugene, OR: Harvest House, 1989).

The Facts on False Teachings in the Church, (Eugene, OR: Harvest House, 1989).

The Facts on Spirit Guides, (Eugene, OR: Harvest House, 1989).

The Facts on "The Last Temptation of Christ," (Eugene, OR: Harvest House, 1989).

The Facts on the Masonic Lodge, (Eugene, OR: Harvest House, 1989).

WHEN DOES LIFE BEGIN?

And 39 other tough questions about abortion

JOHN ANKERBERG & JOHN WELDON

Wolgemuth & Hyatt, Publishers, Inc.
Brentwood, Tennessee

The mission of Wolgemuth & Hyatt, Publishers, Inc. is to publish and distribute books that lead individuals toward:

- A personal faith in the one true God: Father, Son, and Holy Spirit;

- A lifestyle of practical discipleship; and

- A worldview that is consistent with the historic, Christian faith.

Moreover, the Company endeavors to accomplish this mission at a reasonable profit and in a manner which glorifies God and serves His Kingdom.

All Scripture quotations are either from the Holy Bible, New International Version. © 1973, 1978, 1984 by the International Bible Society and are used by permission of Zondervan Bible Publishers, or from the New American Standard Bible, © by The Lockman Foundation 1960, 1962, 1963, 1968, 1971, 1972, 1973, 1975, 1977, and are used by permission.

Back cover photo by Dr. Landrum Shettles; courtesy of Intercessors for America, Reston, Virginia.

Wolgemuth & Hyatt, Publishers, Inc.
1749 Mallory Lane, Suite 110, Brentwood, Tennessee 37027.

ISBN 1-56121-014-5

Dedicated with admiration to our friends
who have devoted their lives
to educating the American public on the
nature of the unborn still in the womb:
Bernard and Adele Nathanson,
Susan Smith, Joe Scheidler,
Judie Brown, Randall Terry

*And to the unborn
who will not walk this earth*

CONTENTS

SECTION 2 — ANSWERING THE CASE WHICH PRO-CHOICE HAS MADE FOR ABORTION

SECTION 3 — ABORTION: A BIBLICAL AND THEOLOGICAL ANALYSIS

SECTION 4 — ABORTION: WHAT CAN INDIVIDUAL CHRISTIANS AND THEIR CHURCHES DO?

A BIBILICAL WORD TO WOMEN WHO HAVE HAD AN ABORTION

Have you had an abortion? As men, we cannot fully understand what you have suffered or may continue to suffer. But we know there is hope — and true freedom available. Perhaps you have already dealt with this issue in your life and are at peace. Perhaps the experience has been suppressed and will only be dealt with at some future point.

Wherever you are, we want you to know that genuine forgiveness and inner peace are possible, that real freedom from the past can be experienced.

If you never have before, perhaps now is the time to deal with this issue — once and for all.

How? Two simple facts should be accepted. One is negative; the other is positive.

First, the negative. Whatever you may choose to think about your abortion, it did take the life of an unborn child. This is an undeniable fact and must sooner or later be accepted. Because it did take another human life, it was wrong. The guilt that many feel is present because they intuitively know what was done was wrong. If it were not so, they would not feel guilt.

But unless the guilt is dealt with once and for all, you and others may continue to suffer its consequences.

Now the positive. This guilt can be removed. What is needed is God's forgiveness. If you truly have this, then you can truly forgive yourself. Then you can experience substantial freedom.

Why is God's forgiveness so important? Because He is the final Court in the universe. If God forgives you once for all, forever, then you are irreversibly and unchangeably forgiven. And only this knowledge—the fact of absolute, complete forgiveness—can set in motion the emotional healing process that will bring real freedom from the past.

But is God willing to forgive? Yes, freely and abundantly if you will admit to Him that you have broken His moral laws. How do we know He will forgive? Because God has said so in the Bible. Repeatedly. Consider the following Scriptures:

. . . but you are a forgiving God, gracious and compassionate, slow to anger and abounding in love. (Nehemiah 9:17b)

You are kind and forgiving , O Lord, abounding in love to all who call to you. (Psalms 86:5)

As far as the east is from the west, so far has he removed our transgressions from us. (Psalms 103:12)

If you, O Lord, kept a record of sins, O Lord, who could stand? But with you there is forgiveness; therefore you are feared. (Psalms 130:3-4)

He who conceals his transgressions does not prosper, but whoever confesses and renounces them finds mercy. (Proverbs 28:13)

"Come now, let us reason together," says the Lord. "Though your sins are like scarlet, they shall be as white as snow." (Isaiah 1:18a; cf. Daniel 9:9)

So if the Son sets you free, you will be free indeed. (John 8:36)

In him [Jesus] we have redemption through his blood, the forgiveness of sins, in accordance with the riches of God's
grace. (Ephesians 1:7)

In fact, God not only forgives, He actually "forgets":

I, even I, am he who blots out your transgressions, for my
own sake, and remembers your sins no more. (Isaiah 43:25)

For I will forgive their wickedness and will remember their
sins no more. (Hebrews 8:12)

All of the above is the basis upon which the Apostle Paul
can encourage us to forget the past completely. Paul, who had
even helped to murder a man called Stephen, experienced many
of the guilt feelings you have felt, but Paul also came to realize
and experience how complete and total God's forgiveness was.
After he experienced God's forgiveness, he knew beyond any
doubt it was God's will that he put the failures of his past behind him and press on: "Brethren, I do not regard myself as
having laid hold of it yet; but one thing I do: forgetting what lies
behind and reaching forward to what lies ahead . . ."
(Philippians 3:13).

But how does one find God's forgiveness? How can one be
certain one is forgiven? Such forgiveness is something that God
is willing to give to any person, whatever wrongs he or she has
done. Abortion is one wrong, one sin, among many.

But all sins need forgiveness. This is why Jesus Christ,
God's Son, came into this world. He was born to die — for us —
to freely pay the divine penalty for the wrongs and sins which
each of us has done, which grieve and separate us from God in
heaven. Because God loved us, He sent Jesus to be punished for
our sins on the cross: "For God so loved the world that he gave
his one and only Son, that whoever believes in him shall not
perish but have eternal life" (John 3:16).

You can find forgiveness right now simply by trusting in
Jesus Christ. You can trust in Christ by turning from your own

ways, acknowledging and confessing your wrongs or sins, and turning to Christ with the confidence that through His power, He will give you forgiveness and new life. If you desire to have your sins forgiven, to be free of guilt, to have new life in Christ and to know God, to know you are loved by Him, the following prayer is suggested:

> Dear God—I do confess my sin. My abortion was wrong and I now come to You asking for Your forgiveness and cleansing. I ask that You will not only forgive this sin, but will forgive all the sins of my life. I accept that Jesus Christ is God, that He died on the cross to pay the penalty for my sins, was resurrected on the third day, and is living today. I now receive Him as my Lord and Savior. I now accept the forgiveness that You so freely provided on the cross and promised me in the Bible. Make Your forgiveness real to me. I ask this in Jesus' name. Amen.

The good news is not only that if we believe in Christ, our sins are forgiven here, but it is also that, in heaven, you will be with your child.

Scripture gives us good reason to believe your baby is alive in heaven and that you will one day see him or her (2 Samuel 12:23; Job 3:16-17, 19; cf. Mark 10:13-16).

Further, in Matthew 18:14 Jesus said: "It is not the will of your Father who is in heaven that one of these little ones perish." The word translated "little ones" is *micron*. It applies to children up to reading age or where they can discern between right and wrong. The word *thelema*, "the will of your Father," has to do with the decision using the will. It is different from the word in 2 Peter 3:9 where we read: "The Lord is not willing that any should perish but that all should come to repentance" (KJV). There the word translated "will" is *boulomai* which has to do with desire toward purpose. He desires that all men would not perish, but obviously some do by making a decision to go against the Lord, but *thelemo* in Matthew 18 says that the Lord has made a decision concerning the "little ones" that do not know the difference between right and wrong, that they will not perish.

Finally, your child has forgiven you as freely and fully as God Himself does. Why? Because it is now his nature to freely forgive just as it is God's nature—because he is now with God and "like Him" (see 1 John 3:2).

"The most dangerous place in the world is in the womb."

(Cardinal Sin of the Philippines)

"The fact that abortion and infanticide result in the destruction of innocent human beings cannot, in itself, be a reason for viewing such actions as wrong."

(Michael Tooley, *Abortion and Infanticide*)

"Although every holocaust ever perpetrated is an unprecedented event in its own right, this should not detract from what all holocausts share in common . . . the systematic and widespread destruction of millions looked upon as indiscriminate masses of subhuman expendables.

"The cultural environment for a human holocaust is present whenever any society can be misled into defining individuals as less than human and therefore devoid of value and respect."

(William Brennan, *Medical Holocausts: Exterminative Medicine in Nazi Germany and Contemporary America*)

"Mental defectives do not have a right to life, and therefore might be killed for food — if we should develop a taste for human flesh — or for the purpose of scientific experimentation."

(Peter Singer, as cited by Martin Maywer in *Fundamentalist Journal*, June 1988)

American Deaths

Based on current figures, by the year 2000, we will be approaching fifty million abortions in the United States alone. In a short twenty-seven years (1973–2000), we will have killed *thirty times* the number of Americans lost in all U.S. wars.

In the table below, the war casualties represent all American combat and combat-related deaths.

Human Deaths Resulting from War and Abortion (Each cross represents 100,000 deaths)	
Revolutionary War (25,324)	-
Civil War (498,332)	✝✝✝✝✝
World War I (116,516)	✝✝
World War II (545,108)	✝✝✝✝✝
Korean War (54,246)	-
Vietnam War (56,555)	-
Modern Abortion Deaths *to A.D. 1990* *(25,200,000)* *to A.D. 2000* *(46,800,000 estimated.)*	✝✝ ✝✝ ✝✝ ✝✝ ✝✝ ✝✝ ✝✝ ✝✝ ✝✝✝✝ ✝✝ ✝✝ ✝✝ ✝✝ ✝✝ ✝✝ ✝✝

WHEN DOES HUMAN LIFE BEGIN?

INTRODUCTION

W hat do you believe about abortion? Have you made up your mind, or are you still uncertain? Have you examined the arguments on both sides of this issue? Are you familiar with what the latest scientific evidence reveals concerning the unborn?

If you are currently a believer in a woman's right to have an abortion, we want you to know this book is written, in part, to you.

We urge caution in reading this book, especially for sensitive people and women who have had abortions. Questions Seven through Eleven are either graphic or may be difficult and painful. We empathize with the pain this information may bring. However, it must be given. For example, concealment of abortion procedures has greatly contributed to the acceptance of abortion.

Both sides of the abortion dilemma acknowledge this is an important, even a vital issue. Even those in favor of an abortion only support it reluctantly — believing it to be the "best" choice, given the circumstances. But is this true?

The answer revolves around the question of when human life begins. Is the pre-born child a genuine human being at any stage of development? Can this be scientifically proven? Let's begin by examining what science has concluded about when human life begins.

WHAT DOES MODERN SCIENCE CONCLUDE ABOUT WHEN HUMAN LIFE BEGINS?

M any people mistakenly feel that abortion is a "religious" issue. But it is not. It is a scientific issue, and specifically, a biological issue. The real authorities on life are biologists. But these are often the last people consulted in seeking an answer to the question. What modern science has concluded is crystal clear — human life begins at conception. This is a matter of scientific fact, not a matter of philosophy or speculation, opinion, conjecture, or theory. It is a matter of simple truth determined by scientific observation and analysis. Today, the evidence that human life begins at conception is a scientific fact so well documented that no intellectually honest and informed scientist or physician can dare to deny it.

In 1973, the Supreme Court concluded in its *Roe v. Wade* decision that it did not have to decide the "difficult question" of when life begins. Why? In essence, they said, "It is impossible to say when human life begins." (99:181; 410 US 113 at 159; cf. 6:81, cf. pp. 73-96; 35:64) The Court misled the public then, and others continue to mislead the public today.

Anyone familiar with recent Supreme Court history knows that two years before *Roe v. Wade,* in October of 1971, a group of 220 distinguished physicians, scientists, and professors submitted an *amicus curiae* brief (advice to a court on some legal matter) to the Supreme Court. They showed the Court how modern science had already established that human life is a continuum, and that the unborn child, from the moment of conception on, is a person and must be considered a person, like its mother (95:19, 29-30). The brief set as its task, "to show how clearly and conclusively modern science — embryology, fetology, genetics, perinatology, all of biology — establishes the humanity of the unborn child" (95:7). For example, "In its seventh week, [the pre-born child] bears the familiar external features and all the internal organs of the adult. . . . The brain in configuration is already like the adult brain and sends out impulses that coordinate the function of other organs. . . . The heart beats sturdily. The stomach produces digestive juices. The liver manufactures blood cells and the kidneys begin to function by extracting uric acid from the child's blood. . . . The muscles of the arms and body can already be set in motion. After the eighth week . . . everything is already present that will be found in the full-term baby" (95:13-14). This brief proved beyond any doubt scientifically that human life begins at conception and that "the unborn is a person within the meaning of the Fifth and Fourteenth Amendments" (95:64, cf. pp. 19-20, 58-64).

In fact, prior to *Roe v. Wade,* virtually every medical and biological textbook assumed or taught that human life begins at conception. That human life begins at conception was an accepted medical fact, but not necessarily a discussed medical fact. This is why some textbooks did not devote a discussion to this issue. But many did. For example, Mr. Patrick A. Trueman helped prepare a 1975 brief before the Illinois Supreme Court on the unborn child. He noted:

We introduced an affidavit from a professor of medicine detailing 19 textbooks on the subject of embryology, used in medical schools today, which universally agreed that human life begins at conception, . . . those textbooks agree that is when human life begins. The court didn't strike that down— the court couldn't strike that down because there was a logical/biological basis for that law. (122:2)

Thus, even though the Supreme Court had been informed of the scientific evidence, they incorrectly concluded there was insufficient evidence to show that the pre-born child was fully human. Even during the growing abortion debate in 1970, the editors of the scientific journal *California Medicine* noted the "curious avoidance of the scientific fact, which everyone really knows: that human life begins at conception and is continuous whether intra- or extra-uterine until death" (97:67).

We will now turn to the scientific evidence that must be the foundation for our thinking on this question. Today, medical texts assume or affirm that human life begins at conception.

For example, Keith L. Moore is professor and chairman of the Department of Anatomy at the University of Toronto Faculty of Medicine. His text, *The Developing Human: Clinically Oriented-Embryology*, is widely used in core courses in medical embryology. This text asserts,

The processes by which a child develops from a single cell are miraculous. . . .

Human development is a continuous process that begins when an ovum from a female is fertilized by a sperm from a male. Growth and differentiation transform the *zygote,* a single cell . . . into a multicellular adult human being." (104:1, emphasis added)

The reference to the "miraculous processes," in a purely secular text, is not surprising. Even a single *strand* of DNA from a human cell, contains information equivalent to a library of one thousand volumes. The complexity of the zygote itself, according to Dr. Hymie Gordon, Chief Geneticist at the Mayo Clinic, "is so great that it is beyond our comprehension" (101:5). In a short nine months' time, one fertilized ovum grows into six thousand million cells that become a living, breathing person like you.

Further, medical dictionaries and encyclopedias all affirm that the embryo is human. Among many we could cite are: *Dorland's Illustrated Medical Dictionary; Tuber's Cyclopedic Medical Dictionary;* and the *Encyclopedia and Dictionary of Medicine, Nursing and Allied Health* which defines the embryo as "the human young from the time of fertilization of the ovum until the beginning of the third month" (105:335).

In 1981, the United States Congress conducted hearings to answer the question, "When does human life begin?" A group of internationally known scientists from around the world appeared before a Senate judiciary subcommittee (85). Here is what the U.S. Congress was told:

Harvard University Medical School's Professor Micheline Matthews-Roth, Principal Research Associate, stated, "In biology and in medicine, it is an accepted fact that the life of any individual organism, reproducing by sexual reproduction, begins at conception" (85; cf. 81:18; 72:149).

Dr. Watson A. Bowes, Jr. of the University of Colorado Medical School testified that "the beginning of a single human life is, from a biological point of view, a simple and straightforward matter—the beginning is conception. This straightforward biological fact should not be distorted to serve sociological, political, or economic goals" (100:114).

Dr. Alfred Bongiovanni of the University of Pennsylvania Medical School noted: "The standard medical texts have long taught that human life begins at conception" (100:114).

He added: "I am no more prepared to say that these early stages represent an incomplete human being than I would be to say that the child prior to the dramatic effects of puberty . . . is not a human being. This is human life at every stage, albeit incomplete, until late adolescence" (100:114).

Dr. McCarthy De Mere, who is a practicing physician as well as a law professor at the University of Tennessee, testified: "The exact moment of the beginning [of] personhood and of the human body is at the moment of conception" (100:114).

World famous geneticist, Dr. Jerome Lejeune, Professor of Fundamental Genetics at the University of Descarte, Paris, France, declared: ". . . each individual has a very unique beginning, the moment of its conception" (85; cf. 81:18).

Dr. Lejeune also emphasized: "The human nature of the human being from conception to old age is not a metaphysical contention, it is plain experimental evidence" (85; cf. 72:149).

The chairman of the Department of Medical Genetics at the Mayo Clinic, Professor Hymie Gordon, testified, "By all the criteria of modern molecular biology, life is present from the moment of conception" (85; cf. 72:149).

He further emphasized: ". . . now we can say, unequivocally, that the question of when life begins. . . . is an established scientific fact. . . . it is an established fact that all life, including human life, begins at the moment of conception" (85; cf. 72:149; 81:18).

At that time the U.S. Senate proposed Senate Bill #158, called the "Human Life Bill." These hearings which lasted 8 days, involving 57 witnesses, were conducted by Senator John East. This Senate report concluded:

> Physicians, biologists, and other scientists agree that conception marks the beginning of the life of a human being—a being that is alive and is a member of the human species. There is overwhelming agreement on this point in countless medical, biological, and scientific writings. (85:7)

In 1981, only one scientist disagreed with the majority's conclusion, and he did so on philosophical and not scientific grounds. In fact, abortion advocates, although invited to do so, failed to produce even one expert witness who would specifically testify that life begins at any other point than conception (100:113).*

Many other biologists and scientists agree that life begins at conception. All agree that there is no point of time or interval of time between conception and birth when the unborn is anything but human.

Landrum B. Shettles, M.D., Ph.D., is one of the twentieth century's titans in the field of embryology and reproductive science. He was the first scientist to consistently achieve *in vitro* fertilization of human eggs. This prominent scientist emphasizes, "The zygote *is* human life" (100:40).

G. L. Flanagan observes, "From their first hour the human cells are distinctly human" (71:12 in 90).

Dr. Margaret Liley and Beth Day state: "A human life begins with a single cell" (71:17 in 91).

Axel Ingelman-Sundberg and Claes Wirsen assert that, "It is a living being from the moment of conception" (71:17 in 92).

World famous geneticist Theodosius Dobzhansky states: "A human begins his existence when a spermatozoon fertilizes an egg cell" (71:16 in 93).

Another leading scientist, Ashley Montagu, confesses, "Every human being starts off as a fertilized egg" (71:16 in 94).

Van Nostrand's Scientific Encyclopedia states, "At the moment the sperm cell of the human male meets the ovum of the female and the union results in a fertilized ovum (zygote) a new [human] life has begun" (96:1087).

All of this evidence is why Professor Jerome Lejeune has stated: "If a fertilized egg is not by itself a full human being, it could never become a man, because something would have to

---

* A few held that life may begin at implantation. However, implantation, while important, in no way defines life.

be added to it, and we know that does not happen" (71:18). Biologically, no one can deny that we are human from conception.

In all stages of our growth, whatever the developing child is called, we are human. At birth humans are called babies. Inside the womb, humans are called "fetuses." Before that, humans are called "embryos." Before that, humans are planted on the uterine wall and called "blastocysts," and before that, humans are called "zygotes." Before that, only an individual sperm and egg existed, and not a human being.

Professor Roth of Harvard University Medical School has emphasized, "It is incorrect to say that the biological data cannot be decisive. . . . it is scientifically correct to say that an individual human life begins at conception, when the egg and sperm join to form the zygote, and that this developing human always is a member of our species in all stages of its life" (85; cf. 81:18; 72:149).

In conclusion, we agree with pioneer medical researcher, Landrum B. Shettles, M.D., Ph.D., that ". . . there is one fact that no one can deny: Human beings begin at conception" (24:16).

Again, let us stress that this is not a matter of religion, it is a matter of *science.* Scientists of every religious view and no religious view—agnostic, Jewish, Buddhist, atheist, Christian, Hindu, etc.—all agree that life begins at conception. This explains why, for example, the International Code of Medical Ethics asserts: "A doctor must always bear in mind the importance of preserving human life from the time of conception until death" (101:317).

This is also why the Declaration of Geneva holds physicians to the following: "I will maintain the utmost respect for human life from the time of conception; even under threat, I will not use my medical knowledge contrary to the laws of humanity" (101:317). These statements can be found in the *World Medical Association Bulletin* for January, 1950 (Vol. 2, p. 5) and April

1949 (Vol. 1, p. 22). In 1970, the World Medical Association again reaffirmed the Declaration of Geneva (101:317).

What difference does it make that human life begins at conception? The difference is this: If human life begins at conception, then abortion is the killing of a human life.

To deny this fact is scientifically impossible.*

Questions for Discussion

1. Who are the experts on when life begins? Why? Is this primarily a religious issue?

2. According to medical and scientific evidence, when does life begin? Why? Can human life be considered a miracle?

3. Knowing this evidence, do you agree with the decision the Supreme Court made in its *Roe v. Wade* case? Explain your answer. Was the Supreme Court sufficiently informed scientifically to decide the issue upon scientific grounds? What do you think they would have decided had they done so?

4. Explain what you understand the following terms to mean: (a) zygote, (b) blastocyst, (c) embryo, and (d) fetus. At what "stage" does human life begin?

---

*   But to accept this fact and maintain that taking human life is not morally wrong is incredible. It is even reminiscent of Nazi Germany and yet today such arguments are increasingly accepted (e.g. 136:16).

HOW HAS MODERN TECHNOLOGY SHOWN THAT HUMAN LIFE BEGINS AT CONCEPTION?

R ecent developments of medical technology such as sound imaging and fetoscopy have permitted us to look into the womb and observe fetal development almost from the point of conception. In terms of what we knew before, the difference is like observing a person's reflection in a pond compared to observing his reflection in a mirror. Modern fetology has given us an incredible look at the growth of the tiny individual in the mother's womb (cf. 139:392).

Dr. Bernard Nathanson discusses how advances in modern technology caused him to radically alter his pro-abortion beliefs. Once known as "the abortion king" because of his prominence in the field and his presiding over 60,000 abortions (46:1189), he is today a vocal opponent of abortion because recent scientific advances in fetology forced him to accept the fact that the fetus was really a living human being:

Ultrasound technology has been really the apparatus which has put the window in the womb. This was the first time we really could see the baby. Up till that time we never could. I mean, X-rays were static. You couldn't really use X-rays to prove or disprove much of anything about the fetus. But ultrasound gives us these very clear, precise pictures, allows us to stimulate the child, see how it breathes, see how it moves, see how it swallows, see how it urinates, see how everything happens.

Now, there's been a new advance in this ultrasound technology which is known as transvaginal sonography. It's very exciting. [Before] the pictures were great, but they don't compare to these pictures—it's valuable for very early pregnancies.

We can see the gestational sac—the little sac of the pregnancy at two weeks following fertilization now with transvaginal sonography. [We] can see the heart beginning to beat at around 3 [to] 3-1/2 weeks now. So this has pushed back or updated a great many of our data about the unborn baby.

And I don't doubt that there are new technologies coming even now; for example, color ultrasound which is going to give us even clearer, more vivid pictures and increase our knowledge about the unborn patient here. (87:7)

Dr. Norman Geisler summarizes the data gathered from fetology in the first five months of pregnancy. In this case we are describing a pre-born girl:

First month—actualization
> Conception—all her human characteristics are present
> She implants or 'nests' in her mother's uterus (one week)
> Her heart muscle pulsates (three weeks)
> Her head, arms, and legs begin to appear

Second month—development
> Her brain waves can be detected (40 to 42 days)
> Her nose, eyes, ears, and toes appear
> Her heart beats and blood (her own type) flows
> Her skeleton develops

She has her own unique fingerprints
She is sensitive to touch on her lips and has reflexes
All her bodily systems are present and functioning

Third month — movement
She swallows, squints, and swims
She grasps with her hands, moves her tongue
She can even suck her thumb
She can feel organic pain (8 to 13 weeks)

Fourth month — growth
Her weight increases six times (to one-half birth weight)
She grows up to 8 to 10 inches long
She can hear her mother's voice

Fifth month — viability
Her skin, hair, and nails develop
She dreams (REM sleep)
She can cry (if air is present)
She can live outside the womb
She is only halfway to her scheduled birth date. (72:150)

The reason why modern science has come to the conclusion that human life begins at conception is because sound imaging and modern fetology have supported this judgment dramatically. Every scientific law known (e.g., biogenesis, i.e., life comes only from life) and every scientific fact (e.g., at conception a genetically new and unique human individual exists) demands this conclusion.

All of this is why human life cannot be defined at any other point than conception.

Questions for Discussion

1. Why is ultrasound and other technology important to the abortion debate? What does it tell us about first trimester abortions?

2. Describe the major characteristics of the pre-born from the first to the fifth month.

3. When Dr. Nathanson changed positions on abortion, he did so solely on the basis of scientific evidence, not religious belief (he remains an atheist). Has the church made abortion more of a *religious* issue than it should be?

WHY DOESN'T HUMAN LIFE BEGIN AT VIABILITY?

I n *Roe v. Wade*, the Supreme Court defined viability as the point when the fetus is "potentially able to live outside the mother's womb, albeit with artificial aid" (99:181; 410 US 113 at 160). In the recent *Webster* decision, the Supreme Court started to reverse itself when it stated, ". . . we do not see why . . . human life should come into existence only at the point of viability, and that therefore there should be a rigid line allowing state regulation after viability but prohibiting it before viability" (51:2).

What is the real problem with viability? Viability is not a fixed concept. It is unreliable in defining the time when a baby can exist outside the womb as a result of the constantly changing technology. Viability itself has gradually decreased from 32 weeks in 1960 to 24-28 weeks or less in 1973 during *Roe v. Wade* (410 US 113 at 160), and now in 1989 it has been reduced to 19-23 weeks. Some doctors believe that in the next 10 years viability will be reduced to 12 to 15 weeks. What will abortionists argue if modern technology learns how to support human life from the embryonic stage? That's why viability is an unreliable concept to define when life begins (51:2-3).

Consider some of the problems with the concept of viability. If dependence on some external "support system" were believed to render an individual "non-viable," then shouldn't we also define everyone with pacemakers, those who depend on kidney dialysis, and even insulin-dependent diabetics as "non-viable"?

Bernard Nathanson observes, "We in the obstetrical community quite simply do not have any reliable tests for viability. . . . Viability is a pathetically unreliable criterion for protection of a human being under the law; there are so many variables and it is so poorly defined that it is all but useless" (51:3).

Significantly, Nathanson observes that if the Supreme Court's recent [*Webster*] definition of viability is the standard to be used, then, to be legally safe, ". . . no abortion is permissible after 19 weeks" (51:3).

Questions for Discussion

1. What does "viability" mean?

2. How did *Roe v. Wade* define viability?

3. If the Court changed its mind on viability and yet based its abortion decision on the basis of viability, what does this say about the original decision?

4. Why isn't viability a reliable concept for determining the protection of a human being?

5. If an artificial placenta is developed, what happens to the idea of viability? Should abortion decisions ever have been made on the basis of viability?

WHY SHOULD WE NOT USE OTHER HUMAN FUNCTIONS TO DEFINE WHEN HUMAN LIFE BEGINS?

I n the last thirty years, many different criteria have been suggested as the basis for determining when life begins, including brain waves, heartbeat, implantation, birth, even social interaction after birth. The problem with these criteria is that there are always cases where such criteria are absent and yet human life clearly exists.

For example, there are many times when people exist without consciousness, without brain waves, without human heartbeat, etc., and yet no one would argue that at that time they are not human.

If we define human life in terms of simple function, that is, certain levels of communication, reasoning, consciousness, etc., we will be excluding many thousands of individuals from the category of "human," including the comatose, the senile, and the retarded. To deny the growing baby in the womb humanity merely because it is now not using certain characteristics of a fully functioning human being (characteristics which are developing but are not at this stage fully in use) is unfair — especially when there is no doubt scientifically that from conception, the pre-born is a human being.

Questions for Discussion

1. Why should we not use such human functions as brain waves, heartbeat, communication, etc., as criteria to define when human life begins?

2. What criteria exist here which are *not* capable of misuse?

Question 5

ISN'T THE FETUS MERELY PART OF THE MOTHER'S BODY?

B iologically, it is a scientific fact that in pregnancy there are two bodies. First, there is the body of the woman. Second, there is another body, that of the child.

Evidence that there are two separate bodies can be seen from the fact that many women carry babies whose blood type differs from their own. It is medically impossible for a single individual to have two completely different blood types.

Another example is a female who may be carrying in her womb a male child. One body may not be both male and female at the same time.

There is also the fact that some women deliver infants which are dead at birth. The infant may have been dead in the womb several days prior to delivery. (Whether it was alive or dead, the infant had its own heartbeat, brain waves, its own fingerprints and its own different DNA structure. Therefore, there has to be two bodies because one body doesn't have two sets of such organs and characteristics.) Also, there are two bodies since one body cannot be dead and alive at the same time.

In addition, the body of the mother recognizes the child as a foreign body. This child would actually be rejected as "foreign tissue" by the woman's body were it not for the protection of the placenta. Doctors tell us that the placenta does not exist until, by its own development, the fetal child triggers the existence of the placenta and places it under his or her own power in order to preserve himself/herself. In fact, the zygote begins to form the placenta within 72 hours!

Professor A. W. Liley, Research Professor in Fetal Physiology in Auckland, New Zealand, is known as the "Father of Fetology." He has stated:

> . . . the foetus is not a passive, dependent, nerveless, fragile vegetable, as tradition has held, but a young human being, dynamic, plastic, resilient and in very large measure in charge of his environment and destiny . . . .

> In summary, the foetus organizes his mother . . . so that nutrients are deflected for foetal needs . . . .

> Throughout pregnancy it is the mother, not the foetus, who is passive and dependent. (101:27, 32-33)

And,

> It is the embryo who stops his mother's periods and makes her womb habitable by developing a placenta and a protective capsule of fluid for himself. He regulates his own amniotic fluid volume and although women speak of their waters breaking or their membranes rupturing, these structures belong to the fetus. And finally, it is the fetus, not the mother, who decides when labor should be initiated. (2:41)

He has also stated, "Biologically, at no stage can we subscribe to the view that the fetus is a mere appendage of the mother. Genetically, mother and baby are separate individuals from conception. Physiologically, we must accept that the conceptus is, in a very large measure, in charge of the pregnancy" (2:41, cf. 24:19).

Further, it is a scientific fact that the little being in the womb has fingerprints, hands, feet, skin, eyes, ears, and genitals that are not the mother's. It has its own lungs, respiration, blood, heart, and circulation that are not the mother's. It has its own mouth, stomach, and digestion that are not the mother's. The growing baby just cannot be shown to be a part of the mother's body.

The fetus is no more a part of the mother's body "than a nursing baby is part of her mother's breast or a test tube baby is part of a petri dish. So distinct is an embryo from a mother's womb that if a fertilized ovum from a black couple is transplanted into a white mother, she will have a black baby" (72:140).

In light of these scientific facts, we may now analyze the leading slogan of those arguing for abortion. Pro-choice advocates argue, "Every woman has the right to control her own body."

Every woman does have the right to control her own body, but she does not have the right to control the destiny of another human being—the baby in her womb. Let's examine the words used in the slogan (2:21-26).

Every woman—At least 50 percent of the babies that are aborted are female human beings. Obviously, then, this slogan is not true for all of these aborted females. If they are part of what is termed "every woman," then obviously they haven't been given the right to control their own body. In fact, this slogan advocates the elitism of the powerful over the powerless rather than equality for all women, as claimed. If all the aborted *women* could return to life, do you think they would agree that abortion is a practice that insures the rights and equality of all *women?*

Has the right—Legally, no one has absolute rights over others. Human life is interrelated in such a way that many individual rights are necessarily curtailed for the welfare of society. For example, no female or male has the absolute right over his or her own body to mutilate it, to abuse it with drugs, to commit suicide, or to endanger the life of others. The same is true concerning human life in the womb. No one has the right to destroy it.

To control—To be "in control" involves the assuming of personal responsibility. But, in fact, it is largely irresponsible actions (e.g., promiscuity) that have led to many pregnancies. Abortion has become the means to protect an immoral lifestyle, to cover over irresponsibility in birth control or to escape the personal responsibility of child rearing.

Her own body—As has already been demonstrated, the fetus is not her own body. It is an independent person—with its own body. This is why Daniel Callahan, Director of the Institute of Society, Ethics and the Life Sciences, has stated, "Genetically, hormonally, and in all organic respects save for the source of its nourishment, a fetus and even an embryo is separate from the woman" (24:19).

Questions for Discussion

1. Is the fetus merely a part of the mother's body? Give four specific reasons for your answer.

2. Who is the passive and dependent party in the pregnancy—the child or the mother? What specific things does the fetus control and accomplish in the pregnancy?

3. Pro-choice advocates use the slogan, "Every woman has the right to control her own body." Do you agree with that slogan? Give at least four reasons for your answer.

Question 6

HOW CAN THE FETUS BE A PERSON?

A bortionists claim that the living human fetus in the womb is not a full person, only a potential person. As such, it is not entitled to constitutional protection as a human being and may be terminated by abortion.

In *Roe v. Wade*, the Supreme Court arbitrarily implied that personhood only existed when the unborn fetus "presumably has the capability of meaningful life outside the mother's womb" (99:183; 410 US 113 at 163). They ruled that "the word 'person' as used in the Fourteenth Amendment does not include the unborn" and that "the unborn have never been recognized in the law as persons in the whole sense" (99:180,182; 410 US 113 at 158, 162). Therefore, before that point (they assumed viability was usually placed at 28 weeks, sometimes 24) a baby in the womb was not yet human (99:181, 191; 410 US 113 at 160, 218).

Of course, their decision is in jeopardy now since viability—the time at which the unborn can exist outside of the womb—has been reduced by new technology to 20-23 weeks and may be 19 weeks or earlier (52:2-3). In the future, as the technology progresses and an artificial placenta is developed, the time of viability will eventually be pushed back even to the point of conception.

Despite the fact that the Court implied personhood as existing at 28 weeks outside of the womb, it allowed babies in the womb to be aborted during the third trimester, all the way up until birth. In *Doe v. Bolton*, the Court allowed a woman to have an abortion anytime during pregnancy if it was to preserve her life or health. The Court defined "health" in the broadest medical context, including emotional, psychological, and family considerations. This allowed any woman the right to have an abortion up to the point of birth if she needed it for her "emotional well being" (99:177, 189; 410 US 113 at 153, 214). Dissenting Justice White correctly summarized the result. Today, abortion is legal in America "for any . . . reason or for no reason at all. . . ." (99:195; 410 US 113 at 221)

What is wrong with the Court's ruling that the fetus is a person only if it can exist outside the mother's womb in a "meaningful" way? What is wrong is that nowhere is "meaningful" defined. Meaningful life to one person may be denied by someone else. Who is to judge? As Richard Exley has written,

> If we base our decision on the prevailing pro-abortion rhetoric, then the unborn baby is not a person unless it is wanted by the mother — unless it is perfectly healthy, free from any deformity or other abnormality.
>
> The problem with that kind of reasoning is that it is based on the subjective opinion of a biased party — namely, the mother and/or the abortionist. Not only does this approach deny the unborn their constitutional rights, it also opens a Pandora's box of potential abuses. (81:30)

To confer personhood by an arbitrary decision or group consensus is reminiscent of an earlier Supreme Court decision that refused to confer personhood on blacks. The *Dred Scott* decision of 1857 declared blacks were "beings of an inferior order," so inferior that they had no rights which white men were bound to respect. (11:284; 2:39) Another example is Hitler's refusal to confer personhood on the Jews. In fact, "Any effort to deny personhood to a biological human being always results in injustice" (75:9a).

For abortionists to refuse to confer personhood on the fetus is an example of prejudice against the fetus.

Once someone denies that personhood is present the moment biological life is present, then he must propose other criteria to define what personhood is. This is where the problem is and this is where a possibility of dangerous abuse occurs.

For example, some apply a "quality of life criteria" to personhood. But this is very subjective and opens the door for social manipulators. Consider the following "indicators" of personality that have been erected and their potential danger for abuse.

One criterion has been to define personhood as existing when complex verbal communication can take place. But this would rule out all babies out of the womb up to the age of when they can talk intelligently. But do we want to allow women the right to kill their infants who are one and two years old? Would this rule permit doctors to kill full-grown adults who are mute, unconscious, or in a coma and who can't talk? Would this allow us to kill the retarded, the senile, those with certain degenerative diseases?

Others propose a criterion of a certain level of consciousness. But this slippery word would put in danger those in a coma, the mentally retarded, and those with certain mental health problems.

Then there are those who propose personhood as a certain level of ability. But whatever that level of physical or mental ability would be, it would rule out those below that level such as the handicapped, the aged, those with certain degenerative diseases, etc.

Still others have proposed such criteria as the capacity to feel pain, to reason, to motivate oneself to a certain level of productive activity.

But would any pro-abortionist argue the above individuals are not persons merely because they do not now meet all of the relevant criteria?

Why must it be assumed that personhood begins at conception? First, because it is a scientific fact that human life begins at conception, and, second, because human life and human personhood cannot be wrenched apart. Third, because every single "indicator" of personhood is not universally applicable.

Another arbitrary criterion is potential life which is said to be different from actual life. If the fetus is categorized as potential life, it can be aborted because it is not actual life. Why is this wrong?

> The sperm and the ovum are not potential life but potential causes of individual human life. They have the potential to cause an individual to come into existence, whereas the zygote has the potential to become what it already in essence is.

> In other words, there is no such thing as a potentially living organism. Every living thing is actual, with more or less potentiality. We are dealing with an actual person with potential, not a potential person. The potential of a human conceptus to know and to love God is an actuality a monkey or rabbit will never possess. (7:52)

How do dictionaries define the word *person? The Oxford American Dictionary* defines *person* as: "an individual human being." *Webster's Third International Dictionary of the English Language* defines *person* as: "an individual human being." In other words, once you have established (as we saw) that the zygote (the fertilized egg) is "an individual human being," you have also established that it is a person. The objective definition of personhood is the dictionary definition, but this is also the biological definition—"an individual human being." Thus, "By objective and scientific criteria, the individual *is a person throughout his entire biological development*" (71:40, emphasis added).

Why then is there so much confusion today over the issue of whether or not the fetus is a person? It is largely because many people have confused the term *personality* with *person*.

Personality must be distinguished from *personhood* since they are not equivalent.

> Personality is a psychological concept; personhood is an onto-logical [property and knowledge of being] category. Personality is a property, but personhood is the substance of being human. Personalities are formed by their surroundings, but personhood is created by God. Thus, personality is developed gradually, but personhood comes instantly at conception. (72:146-147)

Thus, to claim that a human being is not necessarily a person is false. The distinction between *human being* and *person* is arbitrary. *No essential* differences exist between "being human" and "being a person" (72:154).

The real problem is not determining that a human person exists from conception (for us that is established); the real problem is the abuse of the word "personhood" to justify abortions. In a totalitarian approach to personhood, "person" is defined (and redefined) according to the prevailing policy of the state — for state interests. This may even occur in a democracy when the will of the majority defines personhood. But personhood itself is inherent in all (biological) human life. Thus, when human life is present, personhood is present and entitled to full human rights. These rights should never be denied by those who make arbitrary definitions concerning personhood.

We have now shown it is an established scientific fact — which no one can logically deny — that human life begins at conception. We have also indicated that assigning any other point other than conception as the beginning of human life is not only false biologically, it is also arbitrary, unreliable, imprecise, and opens up the door to terrible abuse. Finally, we have seen that from conception onward the individual being must be considered a "person." So what does all of this mean? It means that in abortion we are killing living human beings—human persons—and that no one can afford not to be concerned about this issue. Former abortionist Dr. Bernard Nathanson observes that well before 12 weeks, the fetus "is a fully formed, absolutely identifiable human person . . . indistinguishable from any of us . . . in form or substance" (30:14).

Questions for Discussion

1. Is the fetus a person or a potential person?

2. What kind of criteria are necessary to define what personhood is?

3. What problems arise if we describe personhood as existing when such things as verbal communication have developed? What happens when a certain level of consciousness is required? Do any criteria of personhood exist that are universally applicable?

4. Why must we consider every individual a person throughout his or her entire biological development? On what basis can "being human" and "being a person" be distinguished? Give examples to prove how important it is to acknowledge that personhood is inherent in all (biological) human life, at any stage.

5. How is *personhood* different from *personality,* and what difference does it make?

6. What happens when we allow the state or some other body to define personhood for us?

IS ABORTION MURDER?

O nce we have established that human life begins at conception and that the fetus is a human being, the question
of whether abortion is murder is already answered: The act of
abortion is the act of murder.

Lawyer Mark Belz, head of a St. Louis law firm, observes it
is a fact that,

> Abortion is always an intentional act (at the least, the woman
> and her doctor agree to have the surgery). Thus, abortion is
> by its nature a premeditated act. Once it is established that the
> fetus is a human life, the only conclusion can be that abortion
> is by definition an intentional, premeditated taking of a
> human life. It is not, as promoters euphemistically refer to it,
> a "termination of pregnancy." It is the deliberate killing of a
> human being. (3:18)

But are women and physicians guilty of murder in the legal
sense?

The Model Penal Code, "which serves as a pattern for most
states' criminal laws defines first-degree murder as purposely or
knowingly causing the death of another person" (3:18, emphasis
added). But the facts concerning the fetal development are typically kept from women at the very time they need them. Thus,

most women do not knowingly believe they are purposely causing the death of another person. Given this ignorance, they, too,
are the victims, and for them abortion may not be considered
first degree murder in a legal sense.

But neither does this change the reality of abortion. If a
woman and the father understand she is carrying an unborn
human life, a person, and they still choose an abortion, then at
that point they have violated God's command, "Thou shalt not
kill" and both the man and his wife (or girlfriend) may be considered guilty of the participation in the act of murder or at the
least, some form of negligent homicide.

However, physicians know a great deal more than the average woman. They are responsible to draw fair and accurate conclusions based upon their scientific and medical training. A physician cannot plead ignorance of the facts. Thus, when the
physician performs an abortion, he could be considered guilty of
committing murder. The physician's rationalization that the fetus
is not a person, in spite of his medical training, no more justifies
the act than the acts of the Nazi doctors who arbitrarily determined that Jews were not persons. William Brennan's *Medical
Holocausts: Exterminative Medicine in Nazi Germany and Contemporary America* shows the abuses (98). In fact, there were
carefully reasoned court decisions by judges of the Third Reich
to support and encourage the decisions made by German doctors
(3:20, cf. 98).

Today, why is it the vast majority of M.D.'s refuse to do
abortions (9:261)? One reason is obvious. David Reardon,
Ph.D., observes, "Given the physical and psychological risks of
this surgical procedure, an informed and truly 'conscientious
physician' would almost never prescribe abortion" (9:232).

But there is another reason. If science could conclusively
establish the fact that a fetus is not a person, a human being—
but was just tissue—then there would be no reason at all for any
physician to refuse doing abortions. After all, what percent of

physicians today would refuse to do a tonsillectomy or appendectomy? The reason why physicians refuse to perform abortions is because they know the fetus is not mere "tissue." Their training has taught them that from conception onward they are dealing with a human life. Those physicians who perform abortions must deny or suppress this reality.

But this does not let the medical profession off the hook any more than the rest of us. If physicians *know* that the fetus is more than mere tissue, why then are the vast majority silent while a few physicians continue to engage in the mass slaughter of millions of human beings? If such callous and wanton destruction of human life (26 million) had occurred in any other context (Hitler's Germany only killed 10 million among Jews and other slave labor), those responsible for this kind of behavior could easily have been executed for crimes against humanity. Indeed, "The ethics of abortion, including its slogans, is in principle an ethics of *barbaric totalitarianism*" (11:379).

Lawyer Mark Belz observes:

> We must face reality in America today. An abortion is a murder; abortion is legal; therefore, murder is legal. The entire machinery of the system of jurisprudence in America, since January 22, 1973, has been engaged to promote, protect, and preserve the carrying out of this right to kill. . . . We are witnessing continuous, legal mass slaughter. We must face these facts. (3:24)

If such killings were conducted on any other sub-population of humans, there is no doubt that all parties would be prosecuted and punished.

Questions for Discussion

1. Should abortion be considered murder? Why?

2. How does the Model Penal Code definition of first degree murder relate to abortion?

3. Do legal definitions change what happens in an abortion?

4. Are doctors who perform abortions morally guilty of murder whether or not they are legally guilty? Why do most doctors refuse to perform abortions?

5. Should there be a law requiring women to be informed as to current scientific data on the nature of the unborn prior to an abortion?

6. How do you think people in the future will look back upon the 1973 *Roe v. Wade* decision and its consequences?

7. Do you think modern America may in some ways be similar to pre-Nazi Germany?

WHAT REALLY HAPPENS IN AN ABORTION?

O ne of the major reasons that abortion is tolerated in this country is because people cannot see the procedures and the effects of those procedures upon the little child in the womb. This is the very reason the film "The Silent Scream" (which showed an abortion in the womb) was so controversial and generated such emotion. It visually demonstrated the results of abortion upon an 11-week old girl:

> This film, using new sonographic techniques, shows the outline of the child in the womb thrashing to resist the suction device before it tears off the head. Then you see the dead child dismembered and the head crushed. Then the parts are sucked out. [Note: Because the size of the head is so small in first trimester abortions, suction abortions do not demand the use of ring forceps to crush the fetal head; however, some may employ it as in this case.]

> Nobody who sees this film will speak again of "painless" abortion. The doctor who performed the abortion couldn't bear to watch the film to the end. He rushed out of the room where it was shown and never performed another 'procedure,' though he had performed several thousand before. (cf. 87:7-8)

Those who know what happens in an abortion find it very difficult to condone the practice. The method used depends on the age of the pre-born, although more than one method may be necessary.

When an abortion occurs in the first 12 weeks, as most do, the baby is still small enough to be vacuumed out of the womb by a powerful suction machine—one with almost 25 times the force of a household vacuum cleaner (8:85). In this method, known as suction curettage, the force of the vacuum literally tears or wrenches the child apart, limb by limb, until all that remains is the tiny little head. In any abortion if the infant's head is too large to come through the suction tube itself, the abortionist inserts forceps into the uterus. He uses these to grab the free-floating head, which he then crushes to a small enough size to fit into a suction tube. Then it, too, is removed (81:43).

Dr. Nathanson describes this process, noting, "The baby is simply chopped up and pulled through the suction machine and emerges as just a pile of chopped meat" (87:4). Young states:

> As the suction tube is rotated within the womb, the membrane and fluid surrounding the fetus are quickly sucked away and the little being himself is soon torn apart. Finally the placenta, which is well connected to the lining of the uterus, is pulled away. One manual of instruction describes this phase of the abortion: "At any point that material is felt to be flowing into the tube, motion is stopped until the flow stops. Then the slow up and down gradual rotation pattern is continued. Blood-tinged fluid and bits of pink tissue will be seen flowing through the plastic tubing during the entire suction curettage." (8:85)

Another abortion procedure is called D and E or "dilation and evacuation." The procedure is usually performed during the fourth and eighth months. The cervix is again dilated but instead of suction, the forceps (resembling pliers) are inserted and clamped onto body parts, twisting them off and removing them in pieces. Then the spine and skull are crushed and extracted.

The curette, or sharp, oval shaped knife, is then used to scrape out the uterus.

When D and C (Dilation and Curettage) is used, the knife is repeatedly put inside the womb and rotated. When resistance is encountered, the scraping is concentrated. In other words, a child may have its arms cut off, legs cut off, its face slashed and head cut off and its body mutilated and cut into small pieces. The body parts and placenta are then suctioned out. The technical term for methodologically cutting the baby to pieces is termed "morcellation."

D and E is a very difficult procedure to perform and is potentially dangerous. Dr. Bernard Nathanson calls it "a very dangerous technique in the hands of anyone less than highly skilled" (8:96). He describes the procedure as follows:

> . . . the doctor, with the patient under general anesthesia, punctures the bag of water, drains out the fluid, reaches up into the uterus, finds the baby and then systematically tears the arms and legs off the baby and then takes the parts, the organs, out of its abdomen, pulls the abdominal wall and the chest and the heart and everything else out. And finally, the head is located and crushed with a clamp and removed. (87:4)

Any time an abortion is performed which cuts or sucks the child to pieces, the body parts must be carefully reassembled, if possible, to verify a "complete" infant now exists outside the womb. The reason for this is the danger from infection should any body part of the child be left in the womb. A paper presented to the Association of Planned Parenthood physicians in 1978 described the D and E technique in this manner: "The fetus was extracted in small pieces to minimize cervical trauma. The fetal head was often the most difficult object to crush and remove because of its size and contour. The operator kept track of each portion of the fetal skeleton . . ." (8:96).

The "saline method" (salt poisoning) is another abortion procedure that is used between four and seven months. This was the most common method employed throughout the 1970s (8:89). In this procedure, a 3-1/2 to 4-inch needle is inserted through the stomach wall of the mother into the amniotic sac. Two hundred milliliters of amniotic fluid are withdrawn and replaced with a powerful salt solution. In this procedure the child swallows salt, as well as "breathes" it in. In essence, the child is slowly poisoned while the salt is burning the skin over the entire body. The mother goes into labor and expels a dead, badly burned and shriveled baby. Occasionally, babies survive the procedure and are born with severe complications. Curt Young describes the process:

> Through this process the tissues and organs of the child begin to hemorrhage and are destroyed. Huge bruises appear all over the body surfaces as arteries and veins rupture. When abortionists describe the effect of saline as the "dehydration of the fetus," they have not begun to tell the story.

> Saline has another effect as well. Because the salt is so concentrated, it chemically burns human tissue. The child assaulted with saline looks as though it has succumbed to an attack with napalm. Much of the outer skin has simply been burned away. (8:89)

Other abortions are induced using the chemical prostaglandin. The prostaglandin consists of hormone-like compounds which are injected or applied to the uterine muscle, causing fetal circulatory damage, intense contractions and the expelling of the baby. Because prostaglandin is not as directly lethal to the preborn, such abortions result in far more live births than with the saline method. These unexpected live births are extremely difficult on medical staff and particularly the mother: "Gasping for air, twitching and moving about, babies born struggling to survive abortion are unforgettable to their mothers. After watching these infants die, the scene is replayed mentally over and over again, and a cycle of self punishment may begin" (8:95).

Usually, when the child is born alive, it is simply permitted to starve to death. But there are cases where it is strangled or killed.

In fact, these abortions are so difficult to bear that the "dilation and evacuation" method was developed specifically to avoid the problems of live birth. By cutting, crushing, or poisoning the child to death while still "hidden" in the womb, the results were still lethal but "less visible" to the mother and medical staff. Regardless, the consequences to medical staff remain. For example:

> In Hawaii, McDermott and Char reported that "the nurses themselves felt that they had replaced the illicit underground abortionists in other cities, and, like them, they were personally involved in the slicing and chopping up of 'babies' (the word they used to describe expelled fetal parts and fetuses that were warm and sometimes breathing)" . . . .
>
> Kibel reported nightmares in nurses who had participated in many abortions. . . . He concluded that "regardless of one's religious or philosophic orientation, the unconscious view of abortion remains the same . . . that unconsciously the act of abortion was experienced as an act of murder" . . . .
>
> Physicians are no more immune. Many countries have reported increased depressive reactions and breakdowns among their guilt-ridden doctors. (101:77)

For example, abortionist Dr. William Rashbaum, a faculty member at the Albert Einstein College of Medicine, told the *New York Times* (April 17, 1977) that abortion is the "destruction of life" and noted that for some time he was beset and troubled by pictures of the fetus resisting his attempts to abort it, holding on in the womb for dear life (100:116).

Abortions can also be performed using digoxin (five to eight months) where a syringe filled with digoxin is inserted directly into the heart of the baby, stopping it instantly. It is virtually one hundred percent effective; prostaglandin then induces labor and a dead baby is delivered.

One more method is called a hysterotomy (six to eight months). The only difference between this method and a Caesarean section is that the whole point of the operation is to kill the child, not to save it. An incision is made through the abdomen into the womb, the baby is removed and allowed to die by neglect—or killed by strangulation while still inside the mother (the baby cannot be strangled outside the womb). It's ironic that once the child is outside the womb it cannot be killed; otherwise the physician is legally guilty of murder. Legally, it can only be left to die by starvation.

When one understands what happens to the pre-born infant, and especially if one has seen the gruesome pictures of abortion procedures, one immediately understands that a human person is being violently and mercilessly slaughtered. Pictures convey the reality here far better than any descriptive words can. In fact, simple words cannot adequately describe what occurs in an abortion.

When women later discover what has really happened in their abortion, many are angry and bitter for never being informed of the truth. Further, this explains, in part, the attendant psychological problems experienced by many women known as the "post abortion syndrome" (see Question 12). It is difficult to believe that such acts of violence upon innocent unborn babies have been performed over 26 million times in this country alone. Worldwide, the figure is 50-75 million—per year (143).

Questions for Discussion

1. What happens during the abortion procedures?

2. Are these procedures humane? Why or why not?

3. Knowing about these procedures, would you ever have an abortion? Do you think most women would?

4. How can the church help women who have had abortions and are now dealing with this knowledge?

5. What do you think abortions do to medical staff? Why?

DOES THE BABY FEEL PAIN DURING AN ABORTION?

A s early as 1981, it was strongly suspected by some researchers that pre-born children were capable of feeling pain as early as 8 weeks or 56 days (11:213). (Today this figure may be even lower.)

Dr. Nathanson believes, "I think the baby probably feels pain in all of them [abortion procedures] [although] the degree, the sophistication of the [pain] perception certainly varies with the-length of gestation . . . [but] there's really little question that pain is felt in some degree or other during an abortion" (87:5). Whatever the sensation of pain, there is little doubt that the vast majority of abortions cause pain to the child.

John T. Noonan, Jr., Professor in the School of Law at University of California, Berkeley, describes how these abortion procedures are painful to the pre-born:

> Are these experiences painful? The application of a sharp knife to the skin and the destruction of vital tissue cannot but be a painful experience for any sentient creature. It lasts for about ten minutes.

Being subjected to a vacuum is painful, as is dismemberment by suction. The time from the creation of the vacuum to the chief destruction of the child again is about ten minutes.

Hypertonic saline solution causes what is described as 'exquisite and severe pain' if, by accident during an abortion, it enters subcutaneously the body of the woman having the abortion. It is inferable that the unborn would have an analogous experience lasting some two hours, as the saline solution takes about this long to work before the fetal heart stops.

The impact of prostaglandins constricting the circulation of the blood or impairing the heart must be analogous to that when these phenomena occur in born children: they are not pleasant. If, as has been known to happen, a child survives saline or prostaglandin poisoning and is born alive, the child will be functioning with diminished capacity in such vital functions as breathing and cardiac action. Such impaired functioning is ordinarily experienced as painful . . . .

An observation of Melzack is of particular pertinence: the local injection of hypertonic saline opens the spinal gate, he has remarked, and evokes severe pain. . . . From this it may be inferred that an unborn child subjected to repeated attempts at abortion by saline solution—the baby in the *Edelin* case was such a child—suffers a good deal the first time and much less on the second and third efforts. The general observation of Melzack on the mechanism of pain is also worth recalling: any lesion which impairs the tonic inhibitory influence from the brain opens the gate, with a consequent increase of pain. Any method of abortion which results first in damage to the cortex may have the initial effect of increasing the pain sensations. (11:212-213)

Noonan observes that the later the abortion is, the more substantial and longer-lasting is the pain. It is most severe when the method used is salt poisoning. But he makes another important point. As cruel as such pain is, it is not the real issue. The real issue is the death of the child in the first place:

Whenever the method used, the unborn are experiencing the greatest of bodily evils, the ending of their lives. They are undergoing the death agony. However inarticulate, however slight their cognitive powers, however rudimentary their sensations, they are sentient creatures undergoing the disintegration of their being and the termination of their vital capabilities. That experience is painful in itself.

That is why an observer like Magda Denes, looking at the body of an aborted child, can remark that the face of the child has 'the agonized tautness of one forced to die too soon.' The agony is universal. (11:213)

It is truly incredible that in an age where great amounts of money and effort are expended in saving whales, baby seals, bald eagles, and even three-inch fish — in an era of great concern over "animal rights" — not only do we deny the rights of the unborn to life, we callously turn our heads to their suffering. We not only treat them as less than human, we treat them as having less value than animals. Dogs have more rights in this country than unborn children.

Dr. Irwin Lutzer reveals the twisted and tragic logic of our society which now places a higher value on animal life than on human life:

Nothing dramatizes the schizophrenia of our age more than the law against crushing the egg of a bald eagle. Such a person may be fined $5,000 and put in jail for one year. Incredibly, our society has adopted the notion that a baby eagle is worth more than a human being. Everyone knows that an eagle's egg is a potential eaglet subject to protection, but a fetus, we are told, is not a human being even if it should be already viable outside of the womb. (86:114)

This is one reason why a group of physicians, including two past presidents of the American College of Obstetricians and Gynecologists (Dr. Richard Schmidt and Dr. Fred Hofmeister) wrote to President Reagan in support of disseminating the truth that the fetus does experience pain. They stated:

Over the last 18 years, real time ultrasonography, fetoscopy, study of the fetal EKG . . . and fetal EEG (electroencephalogram) have demonstrated the remarkable responsiveness of the human fetus to pain, touch, and sound. . . . Observations of the fetal electrocardiogram and the increase in fetal movements in saline abortions indicate that the fetus experiences discomfort as it dies. Indeed, one doctor who, the *New York Times* wrote, "conscientiously performs" saline abortions stated, "When you inject the saline, you often see an increase in fetal movements, it's horrible." . . . .

Mr. President, in drawing attention to the capability of the human fetus to feel pain, you stand on firmly established ground. (1:167-168, see 144)

Questions for Discussion

1. Does a fetus experience pain during an abortion?

2. If abortion procedures are painful to a pre-born child, is it fair to describe abortion procedures as "barbaric"? If so, what does this say about society and the medical profession who permit this without protest?

3. Give examples to prove what medical science has discovered about the pain sensations of the fetus.

4. As a society, do we really place more value upon animal rights and suffering than the rights and suffering of pre-born children? If so, why do you think this is true?

WHAT DO SOME WOMEN FEEL DURING AN ABORTION?

M illions of women have now learned first hand what the abortion technique does to their pre-born infant. Some women with later abortions (second or third trimester) tell horror stories of feeling their babies thrashing around, attempting to escape the consequences of the saline poison, the chemicals, or even the forceps and knife.

Physicians know full well what happens to the unborn baby. For example, one doctor who performs saline abortions describes it this way:

> All of a sudden one notices that at the time of the saline infusion there is a lot of activity in the uterus. That's not fluid currents. That's obviously the fetus being distressed by swallowing the concentrated salt solution and kicking violently — [that's part of] the death drama. (81:56)

If physicians are bothered by observing these experiences, what do you think the mothers feel when experiencing the child dying inside of them?

Nancy Jo Mann is the founder of "Women Exploited By Abortion" (WEBA). After seeking an abortion earlier in her life, she realized that she had been deliberately lied to by her abortionist counselors. She was also never informed of the risks. She describes her experience in these words:

> After the fluid was withdrawn, he injected 200cc's of the saline solution—half a pint of concentrated salt solution. From then on, it was terrible.

> My baby began thrashing about—it was like a boxing match. She was in pain. The saline was burning her skin, her eyes, her throat. It was choking her, making her sick. She was in agony, trying to escape . . . .

> For some reason it had never entered my mind that with an abortion she would have to die. I had never wanted my baby to die; I only wanted to get rid of my "problem."

> But it was too late to turn back now. There was no way to save her.

> So instead I talked to her. I tried to comfort her. I tried to ease her pain. I told her I didn't want to do this to her, but it was too late to stop it. I didn't want her to die. I begged her not to die. I told her I was sorry, to forgive me, that I was wrong, that I didn't want to kill her. For two hours I could feel her struggling inside me.

> But then, as suddenly as it began, she stopped. Even today, I remember her very last kick on my left side. She had no strength left. She gave up and died.

> Despite my grief and guilt, I was relieved that her pain was finally over. But I was never the same again. The abortion killed not only my daughter; it killed a part of me.

> Before that needle had entered my abdomen, I had liked myself. . . . When the child I had abandoned suddenly began its struggle within me, I hated myself. It was that fast. Every bit of self esteem, every value I held dear, every hope of which I had ever dreamed—all were-stripped away by the poison of that one vain act. Every memory of joy was now tainted by the stench of death. . . .

There was no way to stop it. There was no way to put everything back the way it had been. I no longer had any control, any choice. I was powerless. I was weak. I was a murderer.

A little while after my baby stopped moving they gave me an intravenous injection to help stimulate labor. I was in hard labor for 12 hours, all through the night. When finally I delivered, the nurses didn't make it into my room in time.

I delivered my daughter myself at 5:30 the next morning, October 31. After I delivered her, I held her in my hands. I looked her over from top to bottom. She had a head of hair, and her eyes were opening. I look at her little tiny feet and hands. Her fingers and toes even had little fingernails and swirls of fingerprints. Everything was perfect. She was not a 'fetus.' She was not a "product of conception." She was a tiny human being. . . . She was my daughter. Twisted with agony, silent and still. Dead.

It seemed like I held her for 10 minutes or more, but it was probably only 30 seconds—because as soon as the nurses came rushing in, they grabbed her from my hands and threw her—literally threw her—into a bed pan and carried her away.

To add insult to injury, after my daughter was taken away, they brought another woman into the room to finish the last hour of her labor. But this woman wasn't having an abortion. No, she had a beautiful, healthy baby boy. No words can describe how rough that was on me.

I was released from the hospital 8 hours after the delivery. The official report filled out by my abortionist stated that the procedure had been completed with 'no complications.' Three days later I went back into what felt like labor pain, and I passed a piece of placenta about the size of my hand. . . . Soon afterwards I began to withdraw from those who loved me, especially from my family since they had supported and encouraged me to have the abortion . . . .

Three weeks after my abortion, I chose to be sterilized by tubal ligation. I couldn't cope with the idea that I could ever possibly kill again. It was too devastating. . . . My body which had the potential of creating life was now too easily a host of death.

I became preoccupied with thoughts of death. I fantasized about how I would die. My baby had struggled for two hours. I've tried to imagine myself dying a similar kind of death. . . .

Four months after my abortion, the bleeding and infection were still persistent. Too ashamed to go to my own Ob/Gyn, I returned to Dr. Fong and he performed a D and C to clean out the uterus. He cut off my cervix and left the packing inside of me. Three weeks later I was grossly rotted out inside.

Seven months later, at 22 years of age, I was forced to undergo a total hysterectomy — all because of that 'safe and easy,' legal abortion. By this time, I didn't care if I lived or died anymore. . . . I hated the world only as much as I hated myself. (9:xvi-xix)

Consider another illustration. Curt Young describes the effect of a saline abortion and its results upon the child: "No one can imagine how excruciating the pain is. We do know that physicians recognize immediately the effect of instilling saline into the woman's gut rather than the amniotic sac. The pain is so unbearable the client may throw herself off the table" (8:89).

This is just what the unborn child does in his mother's womb: he vainly attempts to escape the pain — but he cannot. Again, the mother can feel this. Another mother related the following conversation she had with her doctor:

I went in and I asked, "What are you going to do to me?" All he did was look at my stomach and say, "I'm going to take a little fluid out, put a little fluid in, you'll have severe cramps and expel the fetus." I said, "Is that all?" He said, "That's all."

It did not sound too bad. But what the doctor described to me was not the truth.

Once they put in the saline there is no way to reverse it. And for the next hour and a half I felt my daughter thrash around violently while she was being choked, poisoned, burned, and suffocated to death. I didn't know any of that was going to happen. And I remember talking to her and I remember telling her I didn't want to do this, I wished she could live. And yet she was dying. (8:89)

Questions for Discussion

1. Do some women feel their babies thrashing around during an abortion? In saline, D/E and D/C abortions is there any reason to think a woman would not feel the baby attempting to avoid the procedure? Should it surprise us that any four to six month pre-born would attempt to avoid great pain?

2. Describe some experiences of women who have gone through abortions. Why are you thankful your mother never chose to abort you? Give at least two reasons, one for you and one for your mother.

IS ABORTION A PERFECTLY SAFE PROCEDURE FOR WOMEN? WHAT ARE THE PHYSICAL RISKS?

Most people continue to believe that abortion is a safe procedure — at least for the mother. Those who support abortion in this country constantly inform us that there is nothing to be concerned about. For example, Dr. Jane Hodgson of the University of Minnesota is emphatic that, "[This] is something we ought to be honest about. Abortion is a very safe procedure. There is no question about it being safe. Dr. Koop documented this after months and months of research" (80:5).

But not only is Dr. Hodgson wrong on abortion safety, she has completely misrepresented Dr. Koop. According to many published interviews, Koop believes that abortion not only carries certain *physical* risks, but also believes that eventually serious *psychological* effects will be proven. In essence, all Koop has stated in his famous "report" on the psychological complications of abortion (a 3-page letter) was that the current studies are flawed because they do not examine the problem of psychological consequences for a long enough period (17:30-37; 78:5). In this question we will discuss the physical risks. Question 12 will evaluate the psychological risks.

Compare the above statement by Dr. Hodgson, assuring women that abortion is medically safe, with the following from an official research paper presented to the former U.S. Surgeon General:

> While there are a number of studies with contradictory findings with respect to the medical outcomes of abortion, the following risks have been identified: tubal infertility, subsequent fetal malformations, cervical trauma, ectopic pregnancy, PID [Pelvic Inflammatory Disease], hemorrhaging, infertility, subsequent miscarriages, and death. (Cates et al., 1983, Grimes, 1983, Harlap and Davies, 1975, Frank, et al., 1985, Buehler et al., 1986 [42:5])

After examining "the vast body of the world's medical literature on the subject," Thomas W. Hilgers, M.D., concluded, "The medical hazards of legally induced abortion are very significant and should be conscientiously weighed" (101:58,77).

Hundreds of thousands of women have already paid a physical price and many have paid the ultimate physical price for their abortion: thousands have died. (57; 58; 82; 83; 9:89-114)

Here is a brief list of the possible physical consequences that can come to those having abortions:

- Death

- Perforation of the uterus

- Bleeding requiring transfusion (with possible hepatitis or AIDS infection)

- Tearing of the cervix, with unknown impact upon cervical competence during subsequent pregnancies

- Anesthesia-related accidents, including convulsions, shock, and cardiac arrest from toxic reaction to the anesthetic used

- Pelvic inflammatory disease and possible associated infertility Unintended surgery, including laparotomy, hysterotomy, and hysterectomy

- Bladder perforation

- Bowel perforation

- Persistent bleeding

- Tissue retention

- Anemia

- Peritonitis (a serious infection of the membranous coat lining the abdominal cavity)

- Minor infections and fever of unknown origin

- Undetected tubal pregnancy

- Pulmonary emboli (obstruction of the pulmonary artery)

- Venous thrombophlebitis (inflammation of a vein developing before a blood clot)

- Depression

- Psychosis

- Suicide (33:60-61)

Many women who have experienced such problems are rightfully angry over never being warned of such consequences prior to the abortion. The unfortunate fact is that none of these consequences can be predicted in advance. The woman who has an abortion is playing "Russian Roulette" not only with her body but also with her ability to conceive in the future, with her own mental health, and even with the health of future children (58; 82; 83; 9:89-114).

Here are some official health statistics that reveal the dangers attached to having an abortion. Consider the following data:

Studies show that 20 to 30 percent of all suction and D and C abortions performed in hospitals will result in long term, negative side effects relating primarily to fertility and reproduction. (60:5)

First, every type of abortion procedure carries significant risks. . . . Overall, the rate of immediate and short term complications is no less than 10 percent. . . . The evidence indicates that the actual morbidity rate is probably much higher. (9:93)

The technique of saline abortion was originally developed in the concentration camps of Nazi Germany. In Japan, where abortion has been legalized since the 1940's, the saline abortion technique has been outlawed because it is 'extremely dangerous.' Indeed, in the United States saline abortion is second only to heart transplants as the elective surgery with the highest fatality rate. Despite this fact, state laws attempting to prohibit saline abortions because of their great risks to aborting women have been declared unconstitutional by the courts. (9:96, cf. 140:8)

Frequent complications associated with prostaglandin abortions include spontaneous ruptures in the uterine wall, convulsions, hemorrhage, coagulation defects, and cervical injury. Incomplete abortions are also very common. (9:97)

A high risk of infection is common to all forms of abortion. . . . Many infections are dangerous and life-threatening, and severe pain will typically prompt the patient to seek emergency treatment. But the majority of infections are of a milder order. . . . But long term damage may still result. (9:99)

Studies have shown that a woman's risk of an ectopic pregnancy dramatically increases following an abortion. . . . Treatment of an ectopic pregnancy requires major surgery. . . . [In addition] according to one study, the risk of a second trimester miscarriage increases tenfold following a vaginal abortion. (9:100-101)

Reminiscent of cases of criminal negligence, these women were never informed of abortion risks or else assured that it was a "safe" procedure. That the *image* of safety is vital to the abortion industry for various reasons is obvious—that the essential falseness of this image is usually deliberately hidden is inexcusable. Consider the following:

But as we have seen, the reported immediate complication rate, alone, of abortion is no less than 10 percent. In addition, studies of long-range complications show rates no less than 17 percent and frequently report complication rates in the range of 25 to 40 percent. One public hospital has even reported an overall complication rate following abortion of 70 percent!

The extraordinary degree to which this evidence has been suppressed and ignored is shocking but instructive. . . .

Indeed, the Supreme Court has given abortionists "super rights" which allow them to use any abortion technique they desire, no matter how dangerous it may be, and the Court has made abortion clinics immune from any requirements for minimal standards of counseling.

According to this latter "constitutional right," abortion clinics are allowed, and even encouraged, not to tell their clients any of the risks associated with abortion. Instead, patients are to be kept in ignorance and thereby "protected" from "unnecessary fears" which may lead them to reevaluate the desirability of the abortion option.

The Court guarantees "freedom of choice" but denies the right to "informed choice." *Abortionists can legally withhold information,* or even avoid their clients' direct questions, in order to ensure that the patient will agree to an abortion which will be, they assume, "in her best interests."

Why is there such widespread silence about the dangers of legal abortion? Wasn't abortion legalized in order to *improve* health care for women rather than to encourage them to take unnecessary risks? (9:106-107)

Even the abortion-induced death rates are in all probability underreported and should be of much greater concern. For example:

As with other abortion complications, there is no accurate mechanism for gathering statistics about abortion-related deaths. The Supreme Court's abortion cases have struck down all requirements for reporting abortion-related complications and deaths on the grounds that such reporting might discourage women from seeking abortions. This new freedom allows abortionists and others to disguise abortion deaths under other categories when filling out death certificates. . . .

The degree to which abortion deaths are underreported is hinted at in the results of a 1974 survey which asked 486 obstetricians about their experience with complications resulting from legal abortions. . . . extrapolation of this 6 percent sample rate to all 21,700 obstetricians in the U.S. in 1974 would indicate a probability of 1,300 patient deaths due to abortion-related complications during the six-year period between 1968 and 1974. But the actual number of deaths from legal abortions reported for that period was 52, only *5 percent* of the projected figure. . . . Finally, this projection of 1,300 deaths between 1968 and 1974 is based on a survey of obstetricians only. Aborted women who died under the care of general practitioners or other health professionals would not be included in this survey, so the actual mortality rate, and cover-up, could be even worse.

What should be clear is that there is a major flaw in the mortality statistics for legal abortion. It is quite possible that only 5 to 10 percent of all deaths resulting from legal abortion are being reported as abortion-related. Even if 50 percent were being accurately reported, that extra margin of risk is far greater than women are being led to believe. Indeed, based on the *reported* abortion deaths alone, abortion is already the fifth leading cause of maternal death in the United States.

The most common causes of death from legal abortion include: hemorrhage, infection, blood clots in the lungs, heart failure, and anesthetic complications. These can occur after any type of abortion procedure and are generally unpredictable . . . . more frequently the death occurs after the patient leaves the clinic. . . .

Furthermore, it should be noted that abortion actually increases the chance of maternal death in later pregnancies. (9:109-111)

Subsequent injuries may not be reported for many reasons. Women may attempt this but are ignored or turned away; they previously signed "consent" forms relieving the physician of responsibility for complications (these, however, are not legally-binding); most abortions are personal or family secrets, so most women remain silent about complications and suffer in silence; sensitive gynecologists may not inform a woman her problem is abortion related; finally, it is the abortionists who keep and control the statistics and have numerous motives for not reporting complications, whether immediate or long term (9:108-113). The abortion industry is one of the largest unregulated industries in the nation; accountability is therefore minimized (59; 9:232-272).

What is clear from all of this is that again, no physician in good conscience should perform an abortion: "Given the great psychological and physical risks posed by abortion, it is clear that the responsible physician, when interested in his client's overall health, would be extremely reluctant ever to recommend or perform an abortion" (9:142).

It is obvious that the abortion industry has everything to gain and nothing to lose by withholding data concerning the physical consequences of abortion. For them, to report such information would be like someone turning himself in to the IRS for an audit of last year's taxes and starting out the conversation by revealing a $100,000 bonus that he forgot to report.

Questions for Discussion

1. In what ways are abortion procedures dangerous for women?

2. Name some of the physical risks of abortions.

3. Is any abortion ever risk free?

4. Is it fair never to inform women of these risks?

ARE THERE PSYCHOLOGICAL CONSEQUENCES TO ABORTION?

T he Royal College of Obstetricians and Gynecologists, in a survey of available psychiatric and psychological studies, found that there were serious psychological problems that developed in many women after their abortions. The Royal College reported, "The incidence of serious, permanent psychiatric aftermath is variously reported as between 9 and 59 percent" (9:119).

As noted earlier, Dr. Koop never stated that abortions were psychologically safe. Due to media misreporting, this is how the nation has interpreted him, but falsely so (17:32-33). In fact, Koop has predicted that proper studies in the future will show what he knows personally as a physician—that abortions are dangerous to a woman's mental health (17:31).

Not everyone agrees that Dr. Koop is correct in his assessment that we must wait for future studies to prove abortions do harm. Others believe the data are already sufficient to establish psychological dangers to abortion (78). Even Dr. Koop was concerned enough to admit: ". . . ever since I've been at this job

[Surgeon General] I have been trying to get CDC [Centers for Disease Control] to switch from studying the [abortion] mortality [deaths] to studying the morbidity [physical and psychological complications] which is what this [issue of the "report"] is all about" (17:33).

Even Washington psychiatrist-obstetrician Julius Fogel, a doctor who performs abortions, admitted in 1971 before the Supreme Court decision: "I think every woman . . . has a trauma at destroying a pregnancy . . . she is destroying herself . . . a psychological price is paid . . . it may be alienation, it may be a pushing away from human warmth, perhaps a hardening of the maternal instinct. Something happens on the deepest levels of a woman's consciousness when she destroys a pregnancy. I know that as a psychiatrist" (7:196).

In a 1989 interview he noted (by this time he had performed some 20,000 abortions), "There is no question about the emotional grief and mourning following an abortion. . . . Many come in [to the office even years later]—some are just mute, some hostile. Some burst out crying. . . . There is no question in my mind we are disturbing a life process" (56:20).

What is becoming more and more evident is that whether or not there are immediate psychological consequences, the real psychological consequences to abortion may not emerge until 5, 10, 15, or even 20 or 30 years later.

Dr. David Reardon, Ph.D., a contemporary scholar who has thoroughly researched the subject of abortion, agrees and has stated:

> A woman that a six-month post-abortion survey declares "well-adjusted" may experience severe trauma on the anniversary of the abortion date, or even many years later. This fact is attested to in psychiatric textbooks which affirm that: "The significance of abortions may not be revealed until later periods of emotional depression. During depressions occurring in the fifth or six decades of the patient's life, the psychiatrist frequently hears expressions of remorse and guilt concerning

abortions that occurred twenty or more years earlier." In one study, the number of women who expressed "serious self-reproach" increased fivefold over the period of time covered by the study. . . .

If and when the woman learns that the miscarriage may have been due to a previous abortion, the guilt and anguish can be overwhelming. In this sense, physical complications from abortion often contribute to psychological sequelae as well.

On an even longer time scale, it has been observed that latent anxieties over a previous abortion frequently surface only with the onset of menopause. (9:116)

This whole phenomenon of psychological after-effects which takes place following abortions is known as the "post abortion syndrome" (42:53). Early studies have assumed that this syndrome would appear within a few months after the abortion — but it appears that with the majority of women it can even be 5 to 35 years later. Since abortion has only been legalized in this country since 1973, of course, no one can "scientifically, statistically" prove harmful long-term effects. But the data currently being gathered are more and more pointing to the devastating effects of post-abortion syndrome.

Concerning the psychological complications of abortion, studies show:

- For many reasons psychological complications are more difficult to scientifically prove than physical ones.

- Psychological complications are no less painful than physical ones; they may be more painful.

- The same obstructionism and underreporting found in the area of physical dangers is found here (e.g., 42:8-11). Abortion providers keep few if any records and have vested interests in maintaining the "abortion is safe" myth.

- The studies of abortion advocates are often biased (9:115).

- Studies are usually short term and therefore incapable of revealing long term effects. Immediate short-term studies (several weeks after) reveal lower rates of emotional problems primarily due to the temporary relief afforded by the cessation of the pregnancy or a disorder known as "emotional paralysis" (9:116-117).

Dr. Reardon offers a brief survey of the possible psychological complications due to abortion. We quote:

A European study reported negative psychiatric manifestations following legal abortions in 55 percent of the women examined by psychiatrists.

In the *American Journal of Psychiatry*, researchers reported that of 500 aborted women studied, 43 percent showed immediate negative responses. At the time of a later review, approximately 50 percent expressed negative feelings, and up to 10 percent of the women were classified as having developed serious psychiatric complications.

In one of the most detailed studies of post-abortion sequelae: "Anxiety, which if present after an abortion is felt very keenly, was reported by 43.1 percent . . . Depression, one of the emotions likely to be felt with more than a moderate strength, was reported by 31.9 percent of women surveyed . . . 26.4 percent felt guilt . . . [and] 18.1 percent felt no relief or just a bit. They were overwhelmed by negative feelings. Even those women who were strongly supportive of the right to abort reacted to their own abortions with regret, anger, embarrassment, fear of disapproval and even shame."

In another paper, the same group of psychiatrists reported that when detailed interviews were performed, every aborted woman, "without exception" experienced "feelings of guilt or profound regret. . . . All the women felt that they had lost an important part of themselves."

Another study of aborted women observed that 23 percent suffered "severe guilt."

One doctor reports: "Since abortion was legalized, I have seen hundreds of patients who have had the operation. Approximately 10 percent expressed very little or no concern . . . Among the other 90 percent there were all shades of distress, anxiety, heartache and remorse." (9:119-120)

Abortion cannot help but produce feelings of guilt and depression in most women. But in some women this increases the risk of suicide. Studies concerning abortion and suicide reveal:

Feelings of rejection, low self-esteem, guilt and depression are all ingredients for suicide, and the rate of suicide attempts among aborted women is phenomenally high. According to one study, women who have had abortions are nine times more likely to attempt suicide than women in the general population.

The fact of high suicide rates among aborted women is well known among professionals who counsel suicidal persons. . . . there has been a dramatic rise in the suicide rate since the early 1970s when abortion was first legalized. Between 1978 and 1981 alone, the suicide rate among teenagers [who account for 1/3 of all abortions] increased 500 percent. (9:129)

However, even those who suppress their feelings may also be at risk:

Suppressed feelings of remorse over abortion cause some women to suffer from psychosomatic illness. One study found that self-induced diseases among aborted women included abdominal discomfort, vomiting, pruritis vulvae, dysmenorrhea, frigidity, headaches, insomnia, fatigue, and ulcers. . . .

Abortion has also been identified as the cause of psychotic and schizophrenic reactions. Symptoms frequently include extreme anxiety and feelings of paranoia. (9:130-131)

Although most abortion peddlers promise us that it is the *women* they are most concerned about, it is the women they also may help to destroy. Dr. Reardon's scholarly research reveals:

> Very few women can approach abortion without qualms or walk away from it without regrets. It is this ambivalence towards abortion, to use Francke's title term, which is the gateway to post-abortion sequelae. For most women, abortion is not just an assault on their womb; it is an assault on their psyche.
>
> As we have seen, some women are literally forced into abortion by lovers, families, friends, or even by their physicians. Others slip into the abortion decision, restraining their doubts and questions, simply because it is the most visible and presumably the "easiest" way out of their dilemma. For these women, pro-abortion cliches replace investigation; blind trust supplants foresight. They assume abortion is safe because that is what they are told, and that is what they want to believe. They naively hope that they will have the strength to deal with the aftermath of abortion — even though they are choosing abortion because they feel they lack the strength to handle an unplanned pregnancy.
>
> Unfortunately, abortion does not build psychic strength; it drains it. . . .
>
> The abortion mentality, the institutional system of birth control counselors, abortionists, and clinics, all contribute to this faulty decision-making. As we will see later, abortion counselors are cosmetic figures who only reinforce the abortion choice, acting to support the woman's decision against the rebellion of her instinctive fears against such an unnatural procedure. Rather than urging the woman to confront her decision, reconsider it, and be prepared for its consequences, the counselors work to maintain the "safe and easy" myth and encourage the woman to believe in abortion's tempting lie: "Soon it will all be over." (9:134-135)

Anyone who has examined only a few dozen of the 300 studies conducted on the psychological aftermath of abortion cannot doubt that abortions cause psychological problems to women (42, 58, 82). What is difficult to believe is the irresponsibility of those who claim it has been "proven" there are no psychological dangers.

If so, why are there now tens of thousands of women in groups such as American Victims of Abortion (AVA), Victims of Choice, Women Exploited By Abortion (WEBA), Post Abortion Counseling and Education (PACE), Healing Visions Network and others? Why do hundreds of health care workers attend annual conferences at the University of Notre Dame on post-abortion counseling when there is no need (42:4)?

On March 16, 1989, Congress itself heard testimony of the psychological dangers of abortion from Psychologist Wanda Franz, Ph.D., in a special hearing on the medical and psychological impact of abortion (60:7):

> "Women who report negative after-effects from abortion know exactly what their problem is . . . They report horrible nightmares of children calling to them from trash cans, of body parts, and blood. When they are reminded of the abortion," she continued, "the women re-experienced it with terrible psychological pain . . . They feel worthless and victimized because they failed at the most natural of human activities — the role of being a mother." (60:5)

Other studies, such as the *Report on the Psychological Aftermath of Abortion* (42) released in 1987, concluded:*

> The issue of reporting bias is a very real concern in the examination of post abortion psychological sequelae . . . there is clear evidence of negative emotional aftermath to abortion

---

* Discovery, verification and large scale epidemiological assessment are usually the three phases of research progression. This report noted that in the case of post-abortion reactions only the first phase of research had been conducted, with the observation that the need for phase two has been demonstrated and the recommendation that it proceed (42:8).

from the research results of existing investigations. This is so in spite of either investigator or reporting bias. (42:11)

It is the conclusion of this report that negative psychological after-effects of abortion exist and that they exist on a continuum from mild to severe, and can be the basis of a diagnosed disorder identified as Post Abortion Syndrome. (42:53)

The Report on the Psychological Aftermath of Abortion also revealed in the literature:

The list of psychological abreactions [later responses] to induced abortion is lengthy and worthy of explication [explanation]: guilt, depression, grief, anxiety, sadness, shame, helplessness and hopelessness, lowered self-esteem, distrust, hostility toward self and others, regret, sleep disorders, recurring dreams, nightmares, anniversary reactions, psychophysiological symptoms, suicidal ideation and behavior, alcohol and/or chemical dependencies, sexual dysfunction, insecurity, numbness, painful re-experiencing of the abortion, relationship disruption, communication impairment and/or restriction, isolation, fetal fantasies, self-condemnation, flashbacks, uncontrollable weeping, eating disorders, preoccupation, confused and/or distorted thinking, bitterness, and a sense of loss and emptiness. (42:7)

Further, this report cited several of the same problems found in other reports concerning the reluctance of women to report serious problems:

The post-abortive woman's desire to keep her abortion experience a secret may prevent her from returning to the abortion provider or allowing follow-up to occur. Zimmerman (1977) found that the majority of women viewed abortion as a deviant act, one that they wished to keep a secret. Speckhard (1986) reported similar findings. Of the women she interviewed, 89 percent feared that others would learn of the abortion. . . . In addition, the-post-abortive woman may . . . harbor very ambivalent, if not very negative feelings in regard to their abortion providers following the abortion experience

(Lodl et. al., 1985 and Joy, 1985). Thus, fears of 'being found out,' coupled with ambivalent feelings toward the abortion provider, often result in those women who are most distressed by their abortions being the most unlikely to return to the provider for follow-up. . . .

The delayed onset of many of the symptoms of post abortion stress may cause confusion within the woman in this regard (i.e., as to the origin of her symptoms).

Lastly, there are conflicting interests on the part of the abortion provider which may at times interfere with the provider's willingness to voluntarily furnish the government with evidences of post abortion morbidity. When morbidity data is collected, a well intentioned provider may be reluctant to furnish this information because of an inherent conflict of interest.

Thus it appears that although the federal government does obtain information on abortion morbidity, its data collection may be seriously flawed as to its methodology and findings. (42:6-7)

Finally, the report concluded that the studies with the most flaws are those most likely to report positive outcomes (42:53). Also, it is likely that even the data currently available "underrepresent the extent of the negative psychological aftermath of post abortion" (42:54).

Appendix One of the report cited and described the findings of 90 major studies from 1963-87 which indicated that post abortion psychological problems occur in a significant number of women. Reading through this appendix was sobering to say the least as the different doctors and researchers stressed the serious psychological problems they found resulting from abortion. Here are a few examples of what they said, taken from Appendix One of the report (42):

Clinical report indicating a significant number of women are requesting counseling for a depression problem found to be an expression of unresolved grief over a prior abortion. Most women who chose abortion did so in haste and relative social isolation. (Joy, 1985)

There is a reluctance to call attention to negative consequences of abortion for fear of being seen as providing support to anti-abortion and pro-natalist pressure groups. (Lodl, McGettigan, and Bucy, 1985)

Of 230 women studied, the majority felt "forced" to have an abortion; 83 percent felt 'rushed' to make decision; 71 percent believed their abortion counselors were biased; 80 percent suffered chronic negative psychological sequelae; 19 percent reported suicidal ideation; and 20 percent reported chemical dependencies. (Reardon, 1986)

Found abortion a stressor event [sic] for most women interviewed and that delayed psychological complications occurred for most of the women studied five to ten years post abortion. Eighty-five percent were surprised by the intensity of their negative emotional reactions. Eighty-one percent felt victimized by their abortions. (Speckhard, 1986)

Examined 34 women post abortion. Majority reported chronic emotional problems in the abortion aftermath, including guilt, depression, alcohol and drug abuse, difficulty in relationships, and anxiety in subsequent pregnancies. Twenty-six percent reported making some suicidal gestures since their abortion. (Wall, 1986)

Women with children are more likely to be negatively affected by abortion. Delayed grief was also found. . . . These findings raise questions about the beliefs that only a few women experience post abortion emotional difficulties. (Hittner, 1987)

In conclusion, the promoters of abortion may claim that abortion is always safe, but this is simply not true.

Questions for Discussion

1. Did former Surgeon General C. Everett Koop conclude that an abortion posed no psychological risks to a woman?

2. What are some of the psychological risks a woman faces following an abortion? Are these immediate or long term?

WHAT ARE THE EFFECTS OF ABORTION ON SIBLINGS?

A bortion affects not only the mother and the pre-born (as well as the father and society in general), it may also affect the siblings of the pre-born. This should not be surprising. If the life of a brother or sister in the womb is of so little worth, a sibling may have doubt about his own value. A 1982 study (45) concluded that "children who have siblings terminated by abortion may have psychological conflicts similar to those of children who survive disasters or siblings who die of accident or illness."

Non-aborted children may experience symptoms of the "survivor syndrome"—a combination of anger and guilt. Confusion occurs because their sibling was aborted yet they live; further, the survivor's sense of self worth may be damaged, as well as his perception of parental love (9:226–227). According to Dr. Ney in *Abortion and Child Abuse,*

Abortion diminishes the value of all people, particularly children. When the destruction of the unborn child is socially sanctioned and even applauded, the child can't have much value. More than anyone, children realize they are becoming worth less. Thus, the rate of suicide [among children] has become increased correspondingly. (9:227)

Dr. David Reardon observes some of the specific dangers to children:

The psychological impact of abortion on siblings is significant. In a study of 87 children whose mothers had abortions, researchers found both immediate and delayed reactions. Included under the category of immediate reactions were "anxiety attacks, nightmares, increased aggressiveness, stuttering, running away, death phobias, increased separation anxiety, sudden outbursts of fear or hatred of the mother, and even suicide attempts." Delayed or late reactions included "effects ranging from isolated fantasies to pervading, crucial, and disabling [psychosomatic] illness."

Dr. Edward Sheridan, an Associate Professor of Clinical Psychiatry at Georgetown University Hospital, has provided therapy for abortion-traumatized siblings for the last twenty-five years. His patients range form one-year-old children to adults who are still coming to terms with the knowledge that they lost a sibling to abortion. According to Sheridan, children sometimes become aware of the abortion through overheard conversations, or even by being directly told by their parents. But frequently, even a very young child will "sense" the mother's pregnancy and then become confused when the anticipated brother or sister does not materialize. If no explanation is given, this confusion may lead the child to somehow feel personally responsible for the loss. On the other hand, if the child becomes aware that the mother actively chose to "get rid" of the sibling, he often begins to fear her.

When the child hears mother has gotten rid of baby brother or sister, for whatever reason, this makes him dread things in the home. . . . Mother becomes the agent of death instead of the agent of life. (9:228–229)

Is it really so surprising?

Because the implications of abortion are so clearly hostile to children, a youngster may be disturbed even if the mother has not actually had an abortion. The suspicion that she has, or even would, may be sufficient to trigger anxiety. Consider, for example, the following conversation between a six-year-old girl and her mother who is vocally pro-choice:

Daughter: Mom? Why didn't you abort me?

Mother: Darling? How can you say such a thing? I wanted you! You're my little girl!

Daughter: But what if you hadn't wanted me?

Mother: But I did!

Daughter: But what if you stopped wanting me?

Mother: But I won't!

Daughter: But how can you be sure? What if you do stop wanting me?

This would be an interesting scene to play out and one must wonder how often it has been played out in real life. No matter how emphatically the mother tries to assure the child that she is wanted, the doubts and questions still persist.

If such conversations do not occur openly between mother and child, they may take place within the minds of children. (9:229)

Questions for Discussion

1.   Are there any effects of abortion on siblings?

2.   Name some possible effects of abortion on siblings.

HOW DOES THE USE OF LANGUAGE AFFECT THE ABORTION DEBATE?

B efore we begin our examination of the standard arguments on behalf of abortion, we must first address an important issue relating to the use of language. Many of these arguments offer an improper use, i.e., an abuse, of the meaning of words. This does not increase communication, it increases confusion. Consider the following conversation from Lewis Carroll's *Through the Looking Glass*: "'When I use a word,' Humpty Dumpty said, in a rather scornful tone, 'it means just what I choose it to mean—neither more nor less.' 'The question is,' said Alice, 'whether you can make words mean so many different things.' 'The question is,' said Humpty Dumpty, 'which is to be master—that's all'" (142:1).

Think for a moment how important precise word usage is in science, medicine, theology, etc. It is equally true in the debate over abortion.

The most classic illustration of the misuse of language is found in George Orwell's book *1984*. There, the governmental

"Ministry of Truth" promoted such slogans as, "war is peace," "ignorance is strength," and "freedom is slavery" (89:7).

Orwell foresaw the day when politicians and writers carefully engineered the craft of defending the indefensible. In this gruesome future, language was "designed to make lies sound truthful and murder respectable" (33:53; 89:32). Evans observes,

> Nowhere is this language more widely used today than in the arena of abortion. What "liberation" is there in the destruction of one's own child? What "victory" for women's rights has been wrought doing such violence to the womb? What kind of "choice" is it really when a woman's life-giving, procreative power is betrayed for a mere $250? (33:53)

Even the medical literature today contains Orwellian language. For example, consider the *American Journal of Obstetrics and Gynecology* article (Vol. 161, 1989, p. 446), "Immunoregulatory Activity in Supernatants from Cultures of Normal Human Trophoblast Cells of the First Trimester." Behind the complex scientific title we discover these researchers were describing their experiments on dead babies—on the cells and tissues from aborted fetuses 8-12 weeks old—an experiment, incidentally, funded by our own U.S. government (National Institutes of Health!) (51:6).

The imprecise or even deceptive use of language and promotion of false information has permitted the modern pro-abortion lobby worldwide to increasingly turn the world into a death camp for the unborn: by the year 2000 A.D. the toll may be over one *billion* dead.*

---

* By 1988 over 40 million abortions were performed in Japan (10:267; 9:189). In the U.S. there have been over 26 million abortions. In China 11.5 million abortions are performed each year (32:54).

   In Russia there are reportedly as many abortions as live births. There is not time to mention South and Central America, Eastern Europe, Africa, Western Europe, etc.: worldwide abortions are estimated at 50 to 75 million per year (7:11; 143; 144).

Consider the phrase "termination of pregnancy." This illustration of the misuse of language ignores the reality of abortion. The object of the action becomes the condition of the mother, while the other object (the baby) is completely dropped from awareness. Medical text books use terms such as the *products of conception, fetus ex utero, fetal wastage, abortus, pre-embryo, conceptus, fetal allograft* and others, which are all either impersonal terms or hide the reality of what is being discussed — and often aborted — a living, growing human being who is a person. Abortion clinics use euphemistic titles such as "Planned Parenthood" or "Women's Reproductive Health Center" (43; 77).*

---

*   One tactic of language abuse is to undermine the authority of a position by redefining its rights, strengths, or essential features in a false or negative manner. Thus, peaceful protest against abortion (a civil right) is termed "domestic terrorism." Or, it is argued that because 90 percent of abortions occur in the first trimester, "just tissue" is being removed, thereby justifying the procedure. However, a human being is still destroyed. To argue that a cleaner and more efficient operation somehow justifies abortion (when it kills an individual human being) is barbaric. The destruction is quicker, less visible and less messy than in later abortions: however this only makes the vast number of such operations the more horrible. Further, at the end of the first trimester the child is only slightly smaller than in the picture on the back cover. But even at seven weeks, are we to destroy a human being, merely because it is one inch long (a length each of us once experienced) — or because it leaves no clearly observable human child after an abortion procedure that liquifies it?

Further, in abortions after the 12th week, film and photographs reveal what is actually happening, and cannot be censored by verbal or emotional propaganda. For example, visitors to the German concentration camps in Germany are confronted with the reality and horror of the Holocaust in a way that words cannot convey. In a similar manner, films such as "The Silent Scream" and "Eclipse of Reason" reveal in graphic detail the violence of the abortion process showing what is actually done to the unborn child. They show the gruesome reality of abortion so powerfully that we suspect if women were shown such a film, 90% would, on conscience, refuse the abortion.

In Nazi Germany the Jews were called parasites and nonhuman. In Vietnam the term "selective ordinance" referred to the use of napalm and the term "pacification" referred to bombing raids.

The abortion industry uses the same dishonest tactics today. Language has been incorrectly used to blind America to the reality of what is happening across the nation. Even the new abortion pills that destroy the zygote after conception are termed "post-coital *contraceptives*." (51:7)

Next we present the standard arguments cited in defense of abortion.

Questions for Discussion

1. Why should everyone be aware of the use of language in abortion debates and how language effects the issue?

2. What is the value of learning to think clearly and logically in the abortion debate (or any issue)?

ANSWERING THE CASE WHICH PRO-CHOICE HAS MADE FOR ABORTION

INTRODUCTION

W ith fully one-third of all preborn infants in America today being aborted and destroyed (3:xxi), the fact that there is a growing national controversy can hardly be surprising. Mark Belz, the head of a St. Louis law firm, observes: "We are witnessing continuous, legal mass slaughter. We must face these facts. . . . [But] I fear that most of us . . . have adjusted to the atrocities in our neighborhoods" (3:24, 34)

But many people in America share a different view. They have listened to the arguments of those favoring abortion and concluded that such arguments seem to make sense. They understand the decision to have an abortion is a serious one but they are concerned with the rights of women. They are not convinced abortion is wrong and cite a variety of arguments in defense of their views.

In this section we will attempt to briefly address the arguments they present as legitimate concerns which deserve evaluation, such as: Doesn't a woman have the freedom and the right to control her own body? Isn't the freedom of choice guaranteed by the Constitution a precious and hard-won commodity? Do not rape, incest or severe deformity justify abortion? Is it really fair to expect a victim of such an ugly crime as rape to carry the child to termination? What if the life of the mother is at stake?

Isn't it better only to have "wanted" babies—especially with the current epidemic of child abuse in America? If abortion is outlawed, won't most women be forced into dangerous "back alley" abortions? And won't death rates soar from botched abortions?

If abortion is murder, won't society send women to jail for murdering their children — and then, aren't all women in danger, even from something as innocent as a miscarriage? And doesn't nature itself kill millions of unborn by miscarriage? And isn't the world too populated anyway?

Questions such as these sound convincing. What *are* the rights of a woman with her body? Is abortion taking a human life or not? Is it murder? Shouldn't all children be wanted? What about rape?

Unfortunately, many "pro-choice" people have never critically examined their own arguments on behalf of abortion. Granted, emotional convictions are strong on both sides. But it is obvious both sides cannot be correct. Supporters of abortion are convinced that their decision is sound because their arguments are legitimate. But are they really? In *Bio-Medical Ethics and the Law,* Professor of Philosophy James M. Humber observes that "none of the major defenses of abortion succeeds in its purpose" and "the arguments of the pro-abortionists are all so poor that they should not be accepted at face value, but rather should be seen as after-the-fact rationalizations for beliefs held to be true on other grounds" (136:72, 84).

In this section we will address these issues and speak directly to those who favor abortion.

FREEDOM OF CHOICE – DOESN'T A WOMAN HAVE THE RIGHT TO CONTROL HER OWN BODY?

O ne of the loudest and most widely disseminated phrases of the abortion lobby concerns the woman's right over her body. Does a woman have rights over her own body? Of course she does. On the other hand, she doesn't have the right over someone else's body. The question here is whether or not the zygote, embryo or fetus is truly *her* body. The simple truth is that from zygote onward, the fetus is *not* her body. We have already documented this fact in Question 5 of Section I.

Below we present six additional problems with the "freedom of choice" viewpoint which supports abortion.

A. Are a Woman's "Reproductive Choices and Rights" Really Related to Abortion?

What about a woman's reproductive choices and rights? Are they *really* related to abortion? Given the fact that the embryo or fetus is *not* part of the woman's body, it seems such choices and rights have little to do with abortion:

> Deciding whether to engage in sexual intercourse is the reproductive choice. The ability to make this choice is the [woman's] reproductive right.
>
> Abortion is neither a reproductive choice nor a reproductive right. . . . People have the right to reproduce, and an obligation to exercise this right responsibly. Killing the human being created by reproduction is always irresponsible, and should never be a right. (75:4)

In other words, ". . . if one consents to intercourse, then he or she must accept the consequences which are known to come from intercourse, i.e., the generation of children. When one chooses or consents to have intercourse he or she is thereby implicitly consenting to have children" (68:224).

Abortion then has nothing to do with "reproductive choice." The choice is already made before the pregnancy. Once the woman consents to intercourse and becomes pregnant, her only choice with regard to pregnancy is childbirth or abortion. In conclusion, the abortion choice is, strictly, not a *reproductive* one but a choice of whether to kill the child that resulted from her willful consent of engaging in intercourse (75:4). Morally, any child born of intercourse by consenting parties is implicitly willed and, as such, has the right to live.

B. Is the Human Right to "Freedom of Choice" an Unlimited Right?

Let's dig a bit deeper. The word "choice" is meaningless apart from the object that is chosen. The choice in abortion is whether or not to kill an innocent baby. Since killing cannot be justified, abortion should not be a choice.

"Pro-choice" really means "anything goes." Allowing choices without regard for human life, basic morality or personal responsibility is a recipe for anarchy. Saying "anything goes" regarding the killing of innocent pre-born babies is what 'pro-choice' really means. (75:5)

No one denies that freedom of choice is a right everyone cherishes. But the abortion lobby has twisted this phrase to its own purpose. The freedom of choice does not include freedom to murder another human being. Once it is established that the pre-born child is a human being, then freedom of choice in the case of abortion can only mean freedom to murder. As a society, are we going to allow people to kill other innocent human beings? Well, we already have!

The "choice" is particularly deplorable because 1) the victim is completely innocent, 2) the victim is totally helpless, 3) the order to kill comes from the victim's mother, 4) the order is a reasoned, calculated and intentional act, and 5) the abortionist is paid for the murder (3:24-25).

Consider how many of us have accepted this "right" to abortion without realizing that the very way we phrase it underscores how wrong the argument is. How many people today say, "I wouldn't have an abortion myself but I support the right of someone else to have an abortion"? But would they also say, "I wouldn't own a slave myself but I support the right of someone else to own a slave"? Or, "I wouldn't rape a woman myself but I support the right of others to do so"? Or, "I wouldn't rob a bank, or kill a policeman who inconveniences me, but I support the right of others to do so"?

As Bernard Nathanson has said,

Civilized societies do not permit women absolute control over their bodies; they do not sanction such things as mutilation of one's own body, drug abuse, prostitution, or suicide. Even if (the fetus) is to be considered merely a woman's 'property' and not the 'person' that the anti-abortionists claim, control over property is not absolute—statutes against cruelty to ani-

mals are legitimate, including the animals that the violator
owns. (54:203-204)

C. Are Women Really Free to Choose or More Often Pressured into Having an Abortion?

Several studies reveal that most women, far from exercising a
freely chosen right, feel pressured to have an abortion. For example, "Altogether, fully 64 percent of the aborted women surveyed described themselves as 'forced' into abortion because of
their particular circumstances at that time. . . . Abortion was
simply the most obvious and fastest way to escape from their
dilemmas. Over 84 percent state that they would have kept their
babies 'under better circumstances'" (9:10).

When family and friends, husbands or boyfriends, social
workers, Planned Parenthood counselors and feminists pressure
or intimidate women into having an abortion against their first
choice and best interests, how are they "free" to choose? In fact,
how many parents, even Christian parents, have pressured their
own daughters into having an abortion merely to cover their
child's sin and their own embarrassment?

For most women the "choice" to abort is "an unwanted
choice made in despair" (9:136, cf.pp. 27-40, 134). Consider the
reply of one courageous woman who chose *not* to abort despite
the protests and intimidation of all those around her:

> When I was 21 I became pregnant. . . . The first doctor I went
> to assumed I wanted an abortion before I said anything to
> him. . . . The Planned Parenthood worker who first diagnosed
> my condition was incredulous at my decision. . . . And that
> was the beginning of a very long and painful trial by fire.
>
> I lost my friends because they could not "tolerate my stupid-
> ity". . . . Every time I sat down in the student pub someone
> would start: "Why don't you have an abortion" and later,
> "Why didn't you?". . .

Now older and married . . . I often sit and wonder about the future of women like me who say no. I think about the fact that I was 21 and telling everyone to go to h___ was infinitely easier for me than it must be for a very young teenager, who, although she feels the truth of her unwanted fetus' humanity in her soul before she ever feels the first life movement in her belly, must face outraged parents, social workers who have seen too many tragedies to care anymore, and terrified boyfriends. . . . My heart reaches out with compassion to every woman who has had an abortion against her wishes.

True, nobody can legally drag you on the operating table, but they can certainly use social and financial cattle prods to get you there. (7:181-182)

D. Whose Freedom is the Abortion Lobby Concerned About? Are Women Sufficiently Informed to Make a Genuine Choice?

That the pro-abortion lobby is not defending anyone's freedoms except its own is revealed by two facts: (1) its insistent *denial* of a woman's right to know the relevant factors concerning her abortion and (2) the abortion lobby's attempt to "force" their opinion on society in general.

The abortion lobby continues to effectively withhold pertinent information from women seeking an abortion at the very point they need it the most. Indeed, just when they are making a decision to carry their baby would be the time when common decency would dictate that the rights of women be most respected. Yet they are not.

Many times women who consult the counselors of the abortion lobby are typically *not* told the truth. In fact, they are often given insufficient or incorrect information about the nature of the new life the woman is carrying. The unborn child may be described in impersonal or even derogatory terms and the woman may not be informed as to the physical and emotional risks of the procedure (see Question 11). Rather, as we have seen, the woman is often psychologically "coerced" into a decision for abortion.

In what other medical procedure are people lied to about the nature of the operation and then never informed as to its risks? ". . . abortion is the only surgery for which the surgeon is not obliged to inform the patient of the possible risks of the procedure, or even of the exact nature of the procedure. Indeed, abortion providers are the only medical personnel who have a 'constitutional right' to withhold information, even when directly questioned by the patient" (9:234). Abortion then is hardly a "free choice" when women are deprived of information and socially or psychologically manipulated to have an abortion.

Why do those who so loudly defend "freedom of choice" so resolutely condemn "informed consent" legislation? Why have Planned Parenthood and other pro-choice groups consistently lobbied against informed consent legislation? Is it because they fear that when women learn of the potential dangers, of the nature of the fetus and of the violent procedures of abortion (what it does to their baby), that a large percentage of them will decide against abortion (7:179-180)?

In the area of medical procedure in general, but especially abortion, when another life is at risk (the mother's), true freedom of choice virtually demands exposure to all relevant information. But today, even this may be considered "illegal."

E. What About the Choices and Rights of Others Involved in the Abortion Decision?

Women are not the only ones who are being denied their "rights." What about the right of fathers to choose to save their unborn children from destruction, a right that is now denied by the Supreme Court? What about the right of taxpayers to choose on moral or other grounds not to fund abortions through their tax dollars, a right now denied many taxpayers (127)? What about the right of parents to choose to be involved in an abortion decision made by their daughter who is a minor—another right prohibited by the Supreme Court? And last, but certainly not least, what about the right of unborn children to live?

All things considered, it would appear that the vocal defenders of "choice" and "personal rights" are dedicated to making everyone else agree with the choice of abortion—or else. Consider the comments of U.C. Berkeley professor John Noonan, Jr.:

> After the victory of private choice in the Supreme Court the liberty [to abort] was immediately seen to have social implications: it could not be effectively exercised without vast governmental aid.
>
> The consciences of opponents could not be left free if the exercise was to be effected.
>
> Students in colleges were told to pay for the abortions of their fellow students, whatever their conscientious opposition to abortion, or be expelled.
>
> Hospitals founded by persons who abhorred abortion were assaulted by lawsuits to make them provide facilities for abortion or be held in contempt of court.
>
> Doctors who failed to counsel abortions about which they had moral scruples were threatened with money judgments in tort.
>
> Students who wanted to become doctors were interrogated on their beliefs on abortion before being admitted to medical schools.
>
> Towns that wished to exclude abortion clinics were instructed by judges that they must allow them.
>
> Parents who objected to their daughters' abortions were told by judges that their parental rights were second to the [child's] liberty.
>
> Civic hospitals that refused to perform abortions were, from 1973 to 1976, ordered to do so.

The consciences of whole states opposed to abortion were overridden by judges or governors determined to fund and facilitate the practice. . . . The defenders of conscience — the A.C.L.U. foremost of all — recognized only their own consciences as right. The liberty, so peculiarly private and legend, was ubiquitously social in reality. 'Choice' remained the code word. (13:64)

In conclusion, the slogan, "freedom of choice," is meaningless as an argument to justify abortion. There would be no need to defend abortion if it did not seem to be so clearly the taking of a human life. If abortion was clearly not a process of taking human life, it would naturally come within the sphere of the normal exercise of ordinary human rights (6:137).

"Freedom of choice" is merely a ruse, a deception of the abortion lobby. It is wrong because the freedom to live is always a superior ethic to freedom to choose: without life the possibility of freedom of choice cannot even exist.

True freedom of choice is the freedom to do what is right, not what is personally or socially convenient, and certainly not the option to take another human life.

Even many feminists argue that women are only deceiving themselves if they think the freedom to have an abortion gives women control over their lives. What women are doing is forsaking true womanhood to fit into a world that conveniences the sexual aggression of men. Statistics would seem to indicate that it has been upper middle-class men who have undergirded the cause of abortion in this century (9:313-314).

What modern militant feminists need to realize is that when tough anti-abortion statutes were being enacted into law in the 19th century, it was the militant feminists of that day who were

outspoken in their scorn and condemnation of abortion. Their journal, *Revolution,* urged anti-abortion measures upon the New York legislature in 1869. If the practice was resorted to at all, their leader Elizabeth Caddy Stanton said it was because of 'the degradation of women' by men. Abortion, the physicians attacking the practice agreed, was often imposed on women by men anxious to avoid their responsibility for the children they had fathered. (13:48)

Perhaps this is why, even today, a number of feminist organizations are pro-life.

If society grants millions of women the right to eliminate the "demands" of the unborn child upon their time, energy, vocation, etc., how can anyone be certain that a society in the future will not grant the same right *after* the child is born? Are not the child's demands even greater upon the mother *after* birth? Where is the logical basis for assuming the right in one case and not the other?

There is no neutral ground; if we do not *choose* life, by definition we *choose* death.

In many ways, abortion is like suicide. . . . Granting the wish for suicide or abortion is not an aid to these desperate people. It is abandonment.

If we were to legalize suicide and create suicide clinics where counselors would ease people into and through their suicide decisions, there would be no shortage of desperate people willing to exercise their 'freedom to choose.' Suicidal persons would be promised a 'quick, easy and painless' solution to their problems. They would be promised compassionate care and a release from their seemingly insurmountable burdens, their feelings of loneliness and pointlessness. And so suicide rates would skyrocket just as abortion rates have soared in the last ten years. (9:315)

F. If Women Cannot Have Abortions, Aren't They Being Subjected to Forced Motherhood?

The child in the womb is a separate and different entity and not part of the woman's body. Nor is the baby in the womb the woman's property. "Parents are legal guardians of children, never legal owners. Human beings can never be considered chattel, or the property of another. All are 'created equal,' and possess an inherent dignity because they are a part of the human family" (75:6).

Further, prohibiting abortion "cannot be equated with 'forced motherhood'. . . . Once a woman has conceived a child, a new, unique individual human being has been created. Thus, the woman is already a mother; the separate life within her is her child" (75:6).

A woman's rights are not violated by condemning abortion; to the contrary, killing innocent life within her is obviously the greatest violation of another's rights.

Further, between 97 to 98 percent of abortions are done for convenience. Of the 1.5−2 million women a year who have abortions, less than .06 percent (six of ten thousand) of all pregnancies result from rape. (See Question 21 below.)

Questions for Discussion

1. One of the claims which the pro-abortionists make is that a woman has control over "her own body." After reading this chapter, do you agree with that claim? Why do you think this slogan is so effective? Do you think it tends to diminish personal responsibility? Why?

2. Does a woman have control over someone else's body? What does this say about abortion?

3. Are a woman's "reproductive rights and choices" primarily related to abortion? Why or why not?

4. Is the human right to "freedom of choice" an unlimited right? Explain your answer and illustrate.

5. How do family, friends, or abortionists' groups affect women who are experiencing an unwanted baby? How does this relate to their "freedom of choice"?

6. In what ways could women be better informed about the "choice" of aborting or having a baby? Why do you think women are routinely denied information on abortion procedures/risks? Should "informed consent" legislation be adopted? Can you think of any other medical procedure where people are lied to about the nature of the operation and then not informed as to its risks? What does this say about the abortion industry?

7. Should the fathers be able to express their "choice" in the consideration of an abortion?

8. Has the "pro-choice" lobby lived up to its claims of concern over "freedom of choice"? Give two examples.

9. What was the feminist position on abortion in the 19th century and what does this say about the modern feminist position?

10. If women cannot have abortions, are they being subjected to forced motherhood? Why or why not? How does this relate to "reproductive rights"?

ISN'T IT TRUE THE FETUS IS NOT A HUMAN BEING OR A PERSON, ONLY A "POTENTIAL" HUMAN BEING OR PERSON?

W e have briefly shown that for several reasons the fetus from conception on should be considered a person. Personhood and humanity do not grow; they are inherent. They are not something acquired, they are innate. No human being is "more" human than another.

Consider how absurd this argument really is. In *The Beginning of Life* Jerome Lejeune observes:

When people want to discard a baby they say to you it is not yet a baby. It's something which is not that. And they try to build a theory of 'humanization,' saying that in the beginning there is something which is living, something which is maybe a little human, but it is not a human being, and it is with the improvement of it that someday, by a humanization process, it will become a true human fellow.

Well, that's curious, because nobody argues about that when
we are dealing with mice, for example or when we are dealing with cattle, or even when we are dealing with a big pri-
mate like the chimpanzee. Nobody believes that there is a
progressive chimpanzification of a chimpanzee. Why, then,
does he believe that there is a progressive humanization of a
human being? For a very simple reason. . . . When you are
dealing with human beings that you want to destroy, it is difficult to accept that they are similar to you. Then you get into
moral trouble. And that is just the reason why people try to
masquerade the truth by asking questions which have no
sense [e.g., when does human life begin?] because they would
not scientifically ask those questions for any other living system than the system they will to destroy. (75:9-10)

But to consider another line of argument, we cite the conclusions of Daniel C. H. Overduin, a specialist in social ethics,
who argues that the legitimate definition of a person concerns
the natural capacity (life itself, specific DNA, etc.) and not developed capacity (vocabulary, social relationships, motor skills,
etc.) to act like a person. Only a *person* will ever be able to act
like a person regardless of his/her age or development — whether
pre-born or two years old.

*A person is an individual with a natural capacity for these
activities and relationships, whether this natural capacity is
ever developed or not* — i.e., whether he or she ever attains the
functional capacity or not. . . . Neither a human embryo nor a
rabbit embryo has the functional capacity to think, will, desire, read, and write. The radical difference, from the very
beginning of development, is that *the human embryo actually
has the natural capacity to act in these ways, whereas the
rabbit embryo does not and never will.* (11:347-348, emphasis
added)

These statements indicate the zygote-fetus is not a "potential
person" because 1) it is alive (not potentially alive); because 2)
it has a unique human nature (not a potential human nature); and
because 3) at any stage of development it is most accurately

described as an actual person with great potential. From zygote on, genetically and physically, a unique individual exists:

> *Conception is . . . the point from which a genetically and physically unique individual is present and growing. . . .* At any given moment, a whole living substance — be it a peach tree, a rabbit, or a person — either is or is not alive. Once it is alive, it is totally there as this particular actual being, even though it is only partially there as a *developed* actuality. *There is no such thing as a potentially living organism.* (11:349-350, emphasis added)

In addition, the zygote is a person because it can evolve into nothing else; the essence of its personhood already exists:

> No individual living body can 'become' a person unless it already is a person. *No living being can become anything other than what it already essentially is. . . . Only artifacts, such as clocks and spaceships, come into existence part by part. Living beings come into existence all at once and then gradually unfold to themselves and to the world what they already, but only incipiently, are.* Some developmentalists use the analogy of the blueprint in characterizing the zygote. But a blueprint never becomes part of a house, unless it is used to paper the walls. (11:351, 354, emphasis added)

Overduin proceeds to reveal the underlying "reductionistic" nature of contemporary thinking concerning the unborn. Oversimplified, reductionism would, for example, "reduce" a man to his most fundamental elements, little more than a few dollars worth of chemicals. But human society, for the most part, believes that men are of much more value than their basic chemical parts. Why shouldn't this remain true down to the level of the zygote? Isn't the zygote far more than simply a genetic package?

> Moreover, *the human zygote is much more than a genetic package.* It is a living being which has genes. We do not think that an adult is a package of organs, muscles, and

bones, but that he or she is a being who *has* these structures. The whole of a living being is always, at every stage, much more than the sum of its parts. (11:354, emphasis added)

Finally, we must first recognize the erroneous scientific and philosophical assumptions being presented to define or describe the unborn. Second, be aware of where such erroneous approaches will lead society, and the implications for us all. *A false definition of human life and personhood at any point can become the basis for denying human life and personhood at any point:*

Pre-birth individuals *are now being dehumanized by definition* by quasi-scientific and erroneous philosophical endeavors. . . . sexual utilitarianism tends to keep *the genuine features of early personhood in the dark.* . . . Because the being of a person is, as it were, a seamless robe, our thinking must be woven from the natural substantive and nonfunctional [i.e. essential] level of meaning. Otherwise, 'quality of life' ethics [defining human life to exist at the point of viability, brain waves, consciousness, motor skills] *becomes the survival of the fittest* and of the most functional. (11:355, emphasis added)

It is this kind of popular thinking which causes us to assume that the fetus is something non-human, not a living person at all. The logical consequences of this thinking has produced a new form of prejudice:

Natalism, [which is] the superiority of the born over the unborn, has replaced racism and sexism as the chief atrocity of our time. Fallacious thinking is polluting the atmosphere of thought regarding what a person is and when he or she begins. The philosophical forces of materialism, utilitarianism, and secular humanism press upon every pro-life thinker. (11:355)

Unless society legally accepts personhood from the time of conception, none of us will be safe:

One must not create a legal definition of personhood which flies in the face of medical evidence as to what a person in fact is. In National Socialist law, the Jew — regardless of genetic evidence of his humanity — was deprived of his legal personhood and destroyed like worthless offal. Prior to the American Civil War and the antislavery Amendments to the U.S. Constitution, such judicial decision as Dred Scott relegated slaves to the status of legal nonpersons in spite of clear biological evidence of their humanity. Wherever legal personhood has been defined without reference to objective genetic criteria, the door has been opened to the most frightful consequences. . . .

The law must therefore aim at protecting the rights of the unborn from the moment of conception, not merely from some subsequent point of human development. The law must set its face against functional definitions of personhood. People function as humans because they are human; they do not become human by performing human functions. (35:65-67)

Questions for Discussion

1. What difference does it make whether society considers the fetus a human person? Can "human being" and "human person" be separated as far as the abortion issue is concerned? Is there such a thing as "progressive humanization"? Explain.

2. Give some medical and scientific evidence to prove that from the zygote state on, the fetus is a unique human individual. Why is the zygote-fetus not a "potential person"?

3. What do you understand the philosophy of "reductionism" to mean? How could this influence a person's feeling about abortion? Why is the zygote more than simply a genetic package?

4. How can a false definition of human life and person-hood become the basis for social evils?

5. What does the term "natalism" mean?

6. What are some of the logical consequences of accepting the fact that there is a superiority of the born over the unborn?

SHOULDN'T ABORTION BE ALLOWED SO THAT ONLY "WANTED BABIES" WILL BE BROUGHT INTO THE WORLD? (AFTER ALL, WON'T BRINGING UNWANTED CHILDREN INTO THE WORLD ONLY INCREASE THE INCIDENCE OF CHILD ABUSE?)

W antedness" is a subjective emotion describing someone's feelings. "This means that the value of a human life is not inherent, but rests upon the wants or whims of others. Perhaps the homeless are not 'wanted' either. Should we do away with them" (75:19)?

The fact is that some of the world's greatest leaders in science, industry, politics and religion have all been "unwanted" babies. Some of you reading this book might have also been "unwanted" babies—at least initially.

"Wanted Babies"

Pregnancy is a marvelous thing; but in many people it requires some time to adjust. For example, what some busy women might perceive as an imposition at first, given time, will grow into something that is greatly cherished and wanted, indeed loved.

In two reports on abortion, 73 percent and 84 percent of women who were refused an abortion were later happy that the pregnancy had not been ended (12:212). But the abortion industry seems to be geared toward pressuring women to abort as soon as possible since it knows the greater lapse of time, the greater the chance the woman will keep the child.

Exactly how many women later regret their decision to abort is unknown, but it could easily be in the range of millions of women. It is incredible that no studies have ever been done on this important subject. Is this being fair to women?

Is the problem of "unwantedness" a problem of the child? Is not the child the victim of the parents who do not want him? "Is love more compatible with the taking of another's life, or with the giving of one's life for another" (7:162)?

The truth is, all babies should be born wanted because they are human beings. If they are not wanted, it is the problem of the parents, not the child.

Is it really better to have an abortion than to bring an unwanted child into the world? For whom is it better? Is it better for the mother, who may later decide she wanted the child, or who may encounter psychological consequences? Is it better for the child, who may literally be sliced to death, poisoned, burned, or sucked out of the womb?

Should it really be a national policy to destroy our children merely because they are inconvenient or a burden or "unwanted"? Would we allow this ethic in other areas? For example, when a husband says he no longer wants his mate, do we counsel him to destroy his wife as the most loving thing that can be done?

How ironic! For years women have protested being viewed as objects, the property of a male, and thus disposable when inconvenient and unwanted. Now, when womanhood has finally achieved a voice, some are using it to demand, in the same chauvinism which they deplore, a legal right allowing them to dispose of others in the human family when those in their turn become inconvenient and unwanted. (2:32)

Furthermore, the basic moral question does not have to do with whether or not the baby was *wanted* but with whether or not it was *willed*. Men do not necessarily want many things which they do will. Therefore, they are responsible for these acts. The drunk does not want a hangover even though he did *will* to get drunk. The unwillingness to accept the moral responsibility of one's choices does not lessen the responsibility for them. In other words, if one consents to intercourse then he must accept the consequences which are known to come from intercourse, viz., the generation of offspring. . . . When one chooses or consents to have intercourse, he is thereby implicitly consenting to have children . . . In brief, any child born of intercourse by consenting parties is implicitly willed and as such has the right to live. Abortion does not solve the problem of unwanted children; rather, it compounds the problem. Two wrongs do not make a right. (68:224-225)

Does Abortion Prevent Future Child Abuse?

A related argument of the abortion lobby is that to bring millions of unwanted babies into the world will vastly increase the victims of child abuse. But this argument is wrong on at least two grounds. First, an epidemic of child abuse has occurred *since Roe v. Wade* made abortion available; and second, the victims of child abuse are very often the *wanted* children, not those unwanted.

Abortion, with its philosophy of dehumanizing children *in* the womb, appears to have increased child abuse of children *outside* of the womb, not decreased it. Since we allowed the murder of our own children in the womb, children outside of the womb have increasingly suffered abuse. We have seen millions of battered children, tens of thousands of deaths and hundreds of thousands of injuries.

"According to U.S. Department of Health and Human Services figures between 1973, when abortion was legalized, and 1982, child abuse in America increased more than 500 percent" (72:140). The same pattern of increased child abuse following legalization of abortion is true in other countries including Japan, Britain, and Canada (9:225).

Dr. Philip Ney is a Canadian psychiatrist who has done extensive work with child abuse cases and believes that "elective abortion is an important cause of child abuse" (9:225). He has discovered that Canadian provinces with the highest rates of legal abortion also have the highest and quickest rising rates of child abuse. Provinces with low abortion rates have low rates of child abuse.

Dr. Ney has, in fact, proposed no less than eight possible methods by which abortion may lead to child abuse, e.g., by decreasing a person's instinctual restraint against the occasional rage felt toward those dependent on her care; by diminishing the social taboo against aggression against the defenseless; by interfering with the initial mother-infant bond, thus diminishing future mothering capability; through abortion induced guilt or depression that interferes with the mother's capacity to bond to a "wanted" child, etc. (75:19-20).

Second, it is ironic that it is the *wanted* children who are most often the victims of child abuse, not the other way around as is suggested by the pro-abortion lobbyists:

Pro-abortionists, however, seem to ignore this fact and instead rely on 'common sense' claims that 'unwanted' children are not only unwanted but are the most likely victims of child abuse. But once again, upon investigation, the opposite is found to be true: *it is the children of planned pregnancies who are most at risk of battery.* . . . The evidence strongly suggests that abusing parents carefully plan and desperately want their children. . . . The evidence linking abortion to child abuse is compelling. Since *Roe v. Wade,* child abuse has increased proportionately with the skyrocketing rate of legal abortions. (9:225-226)

Abortion does not prevent child abuse. In fact, abortion itself is the worst form of child abuse — as witnessed by the film, "The Silent Scream." The description below is of an eleven week old fetus being aborted — if this is not child abuse, what is?:

At the beginning of the film, the child can be seen playing, turning around, sucking her thumb; her heart was beating at the normal rate of 120. When the instrument touched the uterine wall, the baby immediately recoiled, and the heart rate rose considerably. The fetus had not yet been touched, but she knew something was happening.

Then the suction began. The child was literally drawn apart piece by piece; and while this was happening, the child was thrashing around, trying to escape the inevitable. Her head was thrown back and her mouth was open wide in what one doctor called her 'silent scream.' Her heart rate was over 200, and you could see the tiny heart beating rapidly. Finally, the forceps came in and crushed the head in order to remove it. The whole process took twelve to fifteen minutes. (7:193)

Is it merely coincidental that as a nation we have seen a vast increase in general social violence since *"Roe v. Wade"*? Mother Teresa observed, "If a mother can take the child in her womb, what is it for me to take you or for you to take me?" (7:202).

As reported on the TV news magazine, "The Reporters," September 10, 1989, there are at least 3 million *reported* incidents of household violence per year. One can only wonder whether a national callousness toward the unborn is bearing fruit for adults as well.

Does not the abortion holocaust logically diminish the social taboo against attacking the defenseless, the "troublesome," or the unwanted? If society devalues unborn children, does it not diminish the value of born children? To what extent does "abortion on demand" contribute to the problems our "wanted" children face?

Questions for Discussion

1. What problem exists with the category of "wantedness" as it relates to abortion? Give two illustrations.

2. If women were never pressured into an abortion and informed as to the procedures and risks, do you think the number of women who would change their minds would be significant?

3. Why is the issue of child abuse irrelevant to the abortion controversy?

4. Give some statistics to prove that legalizing abortion has increased child abuse. Discuss Dr. Ney's study as an illustration.

5. Are wanted children more often victims of child abuse? How does this relate to abortion?

6. Might national abortion policy have contributed to social violence in general?

ISN'T IT TRUE THAT HUMAN LIFE IS ROUTINELY DESTROYED IN MISCARRIAGE AND IN *IN VITRO* FERTILIZATION?

E ach month a woman's body releases one egg for potential fertilization. Once a zygote is implanted in the womb, chemical and other processes begin which inhibit the process from recurring. This is obviously necessary for the protection of the child, for a womb can only safely hold so many babies.

But if nature, or God, permits the destruction of some zygotes in miscarriage, which are after all, persons, why cannot a woman and her physician do the same?

First, there is no moral imperative that men prevent the natural termination of life. Dr. Norman Geisler asserts that this argument

is not a legitimate ground for abortion. It fails to make the crucial distinction between spontaneous death and homicide. We are not morally culpable for the former, but we are for the latter. There is also a high infant mortality rate in some under-developed countries, but this does not justify intentionally killing these babies. . . . There is no unqualified moral duty to interfere with natural death. Protecting life is a moral obligation, but resisting natural death is not necessarily a moral duty. . . . There is no inconsistency between preserving natural life by opposing artificial abortion and allowing natural death by spontaneous abortion. Both respect God's right over human life. (72:152-153)

Further, many miscarriages may result from a natural process that early rejects deformities so severe that the child would not survive. We cannot presume to know the reasons nature or God permits miscarriage in one instance and not in another. But the fact that some zygotes are lost does not alter the reality or importance of the one which is implanted and survives. Dr. Landrum Shettles, M.D., Ph.D. observes:

> The fact that a significant number of zygotes fail to implant and therefore do not result in pregnancy is seized upon by a few as "evidence" that "even Mother Nature" does not consider the fertilized egg genuine human life, any more than 'she' does the hundreds of thousands of eggs and millions of sperm that are "wasted." To this I can only answer that there are also a significant number of one-year-old infants who will never make it to old age, to puberty, or even to their second birthday. . . . Does the fact that life is interrupted at some point after it has begun mean that it never existed [or that it is valueless]? (100:40)

In vitro fertilization involves the uniting of sperm and eggs in an artificial environment for later implantation into a woman who cannot get pregnant by normal means.

Over 200 *in vitro* fertilization clinics operate in the U.S. Worldwide there are 15,000 *in vitro* births each year. As far as *in vitro* fertilization is concerned, unfortunately, human life is destroyed and this involves an abortion. Because obtaining eggs is a major medical procedure with attendant risks, researchers gather as many eggs as possible, even hundreds. These are then added to a dish of sperm in order to achieve conception. One zygote is selected while the rest are discarded. But the scientific fact is that all the fertilized eggs are individual human lives. We must remember that if zygotes are human life, they should be respected, not destroyed. According to *The Dallas Morning News* (September 22, 1989), Tennessee Judge W. Dale Young ruled that "frozen embryos are human life, not property."

This must be recognized by all parties concerned but it must also be recognized that *in vitro* fertilization can easily occur without an abortion. The objection (apart from medical risk and industry abuses, 33:100-117) is only to the current practice, not the process itself.

The solution to this problem is relatively simple. Researchers should place only one egg in the dish and allow it to be impregnated; the other eggs may be preserved in storage for future use, if necessary. If the sperm and eggs are kept separate, no one can object that *in vitro* fertilization destroys human life.

Questions for Discussion

1. Does the fact of miscarriage justify abortion? Discuss your answer in terms of natural vs. artificial termination of life.

2. What is *in vitro* fertilization? Knowing that fertilized eggs are individual human lives, do you believe that the current practice of *in vitro* fertilization is justified? Is there a solution?

ISN'T ABORTION LITTLE MORE THAN WAR ON WOMEN?

I t is amazing that such an argument could be forwarded; the only war waged is the war against pre-born children — over 26 million dead — 20 times the number of Americans lost in *all* American wars. It is incredibly callous to claim that it is women who are having a war waged against them when the bodies of the pre-born dead would already stretch across the country.

Questions for Discussion

1. Approximately how many pre-born children have been aborted in America? 1,000, 1 million, 5 million, 10 million, 26 million?

2. Is this war on women?

AREN'T THERE CERTAIN "HARD" CASES WHERE ABORTIONS ARE CLEARLY JUSTIFIED?

B efore we proceed to examine specific categories, some general comments need to be made. The "hard cases" are statistically negligible: rape .06 percent (70:173), incest 1 percent (9:202), deformity of the child 2−4 percent (11:45-53; but many cases are correctable), and threats to the life of the mother .06−1 percent (11:86).* The number of hard cases total only two to three, at most five percent of all abortion cases (47; 52; 7:169).

Therefore, it is irrelevant to justify abortion in general on the number of hard cases. First, our attention should be focused on eliminating the 95-98 percent of abortions that are done largely for "social reasons," i.e., reasons of personal convenience.

---

* Figures are approximate.

Second, these rare incidences appear to be argued only to divert attention from the majority of abortions which are for convenience to the hard cases.

This kind of argument is a form of the fallacy known as the "appeal to pity." It's like a boy telling his girl friend he will be terribly depressed and suffer rejection (perhaps mental illness or suicide) if she doesn't go to bed with him. But the argument set forth is simply not the issue. In essence, the idea behind an "appeal to pity" is to make one feel so bad over a situation that one is incapable of thinking clearly.

This was the apparent motive of Jane Roe, the woman in the famous "*Roe v. Wade*" case. Norma McCorvey (Miss Roe) claimed she had been raped, had become pregnant and therefore her abortion was justified (75:3). (Denied an abortion under Texas law, she appealed to the Supreme Court and won the right to an abortion, even though by then she had given birth and placed the child for adoption.) But in September, 1987 she reportedly admitted she had lied when she asserted she was raped (47). In other words, the Supreme Court decided the most crucial abortion case, at least in part, on the basis of a lie.

Difficult circumstances during pregnancy do not outweigh the value of protecting human life. The fact that 2—5 percent of pregnancies are the hard cases should not blind us to the fact that 95—98 percent of all abortions are not because of rape, incest, etc., but merely abortions of convenience. With these preliminary comments aside, we may now examine the hard cases to see if they justify abortion.

Questions for Discussion

1. Are there such things as "hard" cases where abortion should be justified? Are such cases ever argued for ulterior motives?

2. Is there more than one victim in the "hard cases"?

DOES A WOMAN'S RAPE JUSTIFY ABORTION?

I n the case of rape, the woman has been violently abused, and certainly, she must be supported by all possible means. No one will deny that she has been the victim of the cruel violence of another. But does this give her the right to subject the innocent life growing within her to a similar violence?

In his *Aborting America,* Dr. Nathanson observes that even the terrible emotional turmoil of a rape cannot justify the taking of a human life. Neither the intent behind intercourse, nor its moral status can change the value of life: "even degradation, shame and emotional disruption are not the moral equivalent of life. Only life is" (54:239).

If sympathy and concern are due the woman as they clearly are, are not sympathy and concern due also to the human life inside the woman? Why kill the innocent child? Doesn't that child have its own right to live? Why punish the child for what its father did? Regardless of the circumstances, once a child exists, genetically the woman is its mother (75:3-4). Will she at least honor that life within her or further compound the problem by bringing a greater violence upon it and destroying it?

Actual pregnancies resulting from rape concern only .06 of 1 percent of all pregnancies (70:173). To justify the abortions of 1.5 to 2 *million* women a year on the basis of a relatively few pregnancies resulting from rape is surely a case of special pleading! One of the reasons pregnancies resulting from rape is so low is because there are a number of physical and emotional factors which mitigate against a woman becoming pregnant during such an emotional trauma.

> Reasons for the lack of conception after rape include: emotional trauma preventing ovulation, impotence on the part of the attacker, use of contraceptives by the woman involved, and so forth. Moreover, it takes time to conceive. (7:173)

Some who have argued for the pro-life stance have written it is medically possible to prevent conception after rape, although this is incorrect as we will show below. For example,

> If a woman receives immediate treatment with estrogen, conception can be prevented. In a Minnesota Hospital, 3,500 rape victims were treated, and there were no pregnancies. In Buffalo, New York, not one pregnancy has resulted from rape in 30 years. In Washington, D.C., a study of over 300 rape victims showed only one resulted in pregnancy. (7:173)

But estrogen does not prevent the sperm and the egg from uniting, forming the zygote. Estrogen only induces menstrual flow which cleanses the womb. In effect, it keeps the zygote from attaching itself to the uterine wall. Thus, it is another form of aborting the zygote.

Justifying all abortions by appealing to a few cases of rape is like justifying robbery in general by appealing to starving people who steal out of desperation. The old saying, "Hard cases make bad laws" is true. Care must be taken not to establish laws on the basis of a relatively few hard cases.

We need to remember that the child of rape is no less an actual human being than any other conceived child. Consider two persons—one conceived in marriage and one conceived by rape — is one person more "human" than the other? Does one have less of a right to live than the other? Can we justify aborting the children resulting from rape on the basis that we know in advance they will not grow up to be valuable, contributing persons in society?

Think of Ethel Waters. When her mother was 12, she became the victim of rape. Although the family considered abortion, the option was rejected. Ethel was permitted to live and grew up to become a famous singer with a fulfilled life. She has sung to millions of people in the Billy Graham crusades. What if the life of this great gospel singer was snuffed out? In her autobiography, *His Eye Is on the Sparrow,* she admits that although her life was difficult in childhood, she is grateful indeed that she was never aborted. Wouldn't you be?

Both rape *and* abortion make objects of human beings.

"When a woman exercises her right to control her own body in total disregard of the body of another human being, it is called abortion. When a man acts out the same philosophy [using a woman], it is called rape" (2:77).

How does killing the child help the raped woman? Abortion may only bring additional emotional and psychological consequences for the woman, who has already suffered enough.

Questions for Discussion

1. Is rape a "non-issue" as far as abortion is concerned?

2. Why does rape not justify an abortion? Give six reasons for your answer.

DOES A GENUINE THREAT TO THE LIFE OF THE MOTHER JUSTIFY ABORTION?

In the instance of a threat to the life of the mother, again, it is only in extremely rare cases that this situation occurs. The question is, "How are such cases related to abortion?" When the mother's life is at stake, as in an ectopic pregnancy (gestation elsewhere than in the uterus) or cancerous uterus, treatment may be necessary that indirectly kills the pre-born. But does this qualify morally or legally as an abortion? In the attempt to save the life of the mother, if the child dies, the child's death was never intended. Its death was the by-product of an attempt to save the mother's life. In abortion the intent is always to kill (75:3).

The former U.S. Surgeon General C. Everett Koop observes:

Protection of the life of the mother as an excuse for an abortion is a smoke screen. In my 36 years of pediatric surgery, I have never known of one instance where the child had to be aborted to save the mother's life. If toward the end of the pregnancy complications arise that threaten the mother's health, the doctor will either induce labor or perform a Caesarean section. His intention is to save the life of both the mother and the baby. The baby's life is never willfully destroyed because the mother's life is in danger (44:2).

In other words, what is the motive of those justifying abortion? Is using a *possible* threat to the mother's life a reason to end the life of the child or must there be clear and immediate danger of death to the mother? If there is, then preference is to be given to the life of the mother, but when possible all efforts to save the life of the child are employed.

In an ectopic pregnancy, the doctor has no choice. He can either save the mother or lose both the mother and child. If it is truly impossible to save both lives, the doctor should certainly save one. But it should be done only on the basis of a "lesser of two evils" mentality, not one of strict neutrality. But even ectopic pregnancies, although experiencing a 300 percent increase since *Roe v. Wade,* probably due to abortion complications (1:86; 9:100), are still rare (9:100; 11:85).

Questions for Discussion

1. Is abortion justified when there is a threat to the life of the mother? Give reasons for your answer.

2. In what sense is this not an abortion issue?

DOES INCEST JUSTIFY AN ABORTION?

Cases of rape or incest are some of the ultimate tragedies of life. Every decision surrounding these traumatic cases is extremely difficult and painful. An emotionally devastating act has been forced upon a woman or young girl. What are the most helpful things that can be done for her? Now, in her tragedy, decisions must be made. None are easy or uncomplicated.

If she discovers she is pregnant, is abortion the best thing for her to do? Whether she aborts the baby or keeps the baby will not change what happened to her, namely her rape or incest. Recent reports confirm that abortion can be damaging both mentally and physically even in the hard cases of rape or incest. Further, would it not be better for women to lovingly care for an innocent child and provide it a good home either by adoption or making it part of their family? Isn't that the only way that a woman can consistently follow an ethic of loving all children? For example, when she later delivers her own children and looks at them, which decision will free her of guilt at the time? The decision to abort or to carry an innocent child through a difficult pregnancy?

Questions for Discussion

1. Does incest justify an abortion?

2. Give reasons for your answer.

DOES THE POSSIBILITY OF DEFORMITY JUSTIFY AN ABORTION?

M any people feel that abortions should be permitted in cases of deformity (severe or otherwise) — motor or mental disabilities which can be detected in the womb by amniocentesis and other methods. But who among us is able or prepared to ultimately judge the value of a handicapped person's life? If the existence of life is valuable, then even defective life is valuable and better than no life at all.

The vast majority of handicapped will agree — just ask them. Endless numbers of people with endless numbers of abnormalities enjoy life, from polio victims to those born without legs. If we abort the abnormal in the womb, on what logical basis can we not kill the abnormal in their childhood or even adult stage? Genetic screening (the testing of the fetus for physical defects while still in the womb) with a goal toward abortion is more reminiscent of Nazi eugenics than compassion.

Also, genetic screening is not 100 percent accurate — rarely a perfectly normal baby will be aborted (11:49).

In a society that stresses physical beauty, the issue of deformities becomes an unjust one, principally because of perception: what is perceived as unlovely and a burden becomes so, whether or not this is the case. While not minimizing the problems involved with a child having severe motor or mental difficulties, few will deny that beauty is in the eye of the beholder or that couples who have chosen to raise such children almost never regret it; indeed far from thinking the child an unbearable burden — most discover them to be a blessing.

But the statements made by some of our leading scientists and "humanitarians" are frightening. Social engineering is coming closer and closer to social policy. The typical argument is that such people should not be allowed to live on the basis of "quality of life" considerations. Dr. James Sorenson was quoted earlier as noting what must be the ultimate in "doublespeak": "American opinion is rapidly moving toward the position where the parents who have an abnormal child may be considered *irresponsible*" (5:47, emphasis added).

In other words the *responsible* thing to do is to destroy the child and get it out of the way; but, in fact, this is the height of *irresponsibility*. There was a time when the responsible thing was to raise the child as a loved and valued member of the family. The word responsible involves things like being trustworthy, accountable, rational and dutiful. A responsible person is morally obliged to carry out a duty and can be blamed for failure to do so. But today millions of fathers and mothers feel no duty at all to their unborn children. And the abortion lobby and the social engineers call them *responsible* persons!

In the book, *Ideals of Life,* Millard Everett observes, "No child [should] be admitted into the society of the living who would be certain to suffer any social handicap — for example, any physical or mental defect that would prevent marriage or that would make others tolerate his company only from the sense of mercy" (5:48).

Who defines "social handicap"? Who defines "value"? Which of us is not "socially handicapped" to some degree?

The former U.S. Surgeon General, C. Everett Koop, one of the world's leading pediatric surgeons specializing in correcting birth defects, has some important observations. Of the thousands of surgeries he has performed in order to correct such deformities, some with little success, at the end of his lengthy career he is able to state:

> Yet, I have a sense of satisfaction in my career, best indicated perhaps by the fact that no family has ever come to me and said: 'Why did you work so hard to save the life of my child?' And no grown child has ever come back to ask me why, either. (5:44)

He also observes, "Very, very few parents of their own volition come to a physician and say, 'My baby has a life not worthy to be lived' " (5:55).

In one extensive study of families with defective children, Koop observes, "Many of them were better families than they would have been without the necessity of facing the adversity produced by the problems of the imperfect child" (5:44). Koop asserts it has been his "constant experience" that unhappiness and disability do not necessarily go together. In fact, some of the most unhappy children that he has known were "perfect" children, while some of the happiest youngsters he knew carried burdens that most people would find impossible to bear (5:46).

How then can we say that children should be aborted or permitted to die because their lives would "obviously" be nothing but miserable? We do not have sufficient information to make that judgment.

Consider the brilliant physicist Stephen Hawking, who holds Newton's chair as Lucasian Professor of Mathematics at Cambridge University, and is widely regarded as the most brilliant theoretical physicist since Einstein (88). Is Stephen Hawking's life miserable because (due to Lou Gehrig's disease) only his mind functions properly? Is he not what many people today would callously refer to as a physical "vegetable"? And yet has he not made immeasurable contributions to the advance of science? If his parents could have looked into the future but seen only the fact of his physical deformities, would they have decided his life wasn't worth living? Then he would have been destroyed before he had a chance to live and if so, they would have been terribly wrong.

This is exactly the case with many parents today who face the possibility of a deformed child. All they "see" is the physical deformity which outweighs all else. Three additional factors are ignored: 1) the tests are sometimes in error; 2) no one can know the final outcome of another's life, and 3) no one has the right to take the life of an innocent party. No one is God.

One can only wonder how many Stephen Hawkings and Ethel Waters have been among the 26 million abortions in recent years. The moment we let anyone — physician, scientist, society, etc. — make decisions as to our "value" on the basis of any criteria, the door is open for terrible abuses. As far back as 1973, James Watson, the co-worker and co-discoverer with Francis Crick of the DNA helix stated, "If a child were not declared alive until 3 days after birth, then all parents could be allowed the choice that only a few are given under the present system. The doctor could allow the child to die if a parent so chose and save a lot of misery and suffering" (*Time*, May 28, 1973, p. 104; 37:94).

Francis Crick himself argued that "no newborn infant should be declared human until it has passed certain tests regarding its genetic endowment and if it fails these tests, *it forfeits the right to live*" (129:97, emphasis added).

Think for a moment about an article by Leo Alexander, a Boston psychiatrist who was at one point a consultant to the Secretary of War on duty with the Office of Chief Counsel for War Crimes in Nuremberg. In the *New England Journal of*

Medicine, July 4, 1949, he wrote an article titled "Medical Science Under Dictatorship" (5:61-64).

He observed a number of facts in Nazi Germany which bear upon our nation's abortion policies, our acceptance of infanticide and our increasing acceptance of euthanasia and legal suicide (103), all of which are based largely upon a subjective "quality of life" and utilitarian (actions are right because they are useful) assumptions concerning human beings.

Dr. Alexander first points out the basic philosophical premise of recent dictatorships, including the Nazis, was essentially Hegelian: a doctrine of "rational utility" and a corresponding doctrine of social planning which had replaced ethical, moral and religious values (cf. 98).

In Nazi Germany, medical science employed this Hegelian trend. For example, there was mass extermination of the chronically sick. Such persons were impersonalized and deemed unworthy of medical care. Killing such people was justified on the grounds that the state would reap financial benefits and that "useless" medical expenses would be avoided.

Both adults and children were propagandized. For example, the Nazis made a film titled "I Accuse" which depicted the life story of a woman with multiple sclerosis. Her husband, along with a doctor, murdered her to the accompaniment of soft piano music.

In German schools, even the arithmetic books of high school students included problems that were given in distorted terms concerning the cost to society of caring for and rehabilitating the crippled and severely ill. One problem asked students how many new housing units could be built, or how many marriage allowance loans could be given newlyweds for the same amount of money that it would cost the state to care for "the crippled, the criminal, and the insane."

There was also mass propaganda to eliminate individuals considered socially disturbing, unwanted or racially or ideologically "impure." Every person whom the state viewed suspiciously was at risk. Those who were viewed as disloyal or perceived to be "in the way" were exterminated. All human life was stripped of its innate value and people were defined as valuable only if they served the function of state interests. Accompanying this was ruthless experimentation on human beings under such lofty goals as the promotion of medical military research.

We must be aware that it was medical doctors who helped construct these values. Those who had begun their careers sworn to preserve life actually became its destroyers.

Today, in America, some of our own medical profession and those in scientific research are expending considerable time and effort to develop numerous scientific techniques to successfully abort human beings — to "efficiently" kill the fetus at various stages of its life (1:161-165). These more efficient methods that destroy human life are deemed "good"; those which kill are said to be "curative."

Unfortunately, in December, 1989, the American Medical Association itself "took a strong pro-choice stance on abortion" (128).

Dr. Alexander points out that the devaluating of human life came *before* Hitler came to power. This philosophical change came about, in part, because of those in the medical profession. In brief, physicians had already prepared themselves for Hitler's orders. The government issued its first direct order for euthanasia in 1939. By it, every state institution was bound by law to report on patients who had been ill for five years or more and those who were unable to work. The decision to kill was made on the basis of marital status, nationality, next of kin, race, name, visitors, and financial responsibility. The "experts" who made such decisions were primarily psychiatric professors in the major universities of Germany. They never even saw the patients.

There was also a specific organization to murder children known by the euphemistic name of "Realms Committee for Scientific Approach to Severe Illness Due to Heredity and Constitution." The transportation of the patients to the killing centers was carried out by another innocent sounding organization named, "Charitable Transport Company for the Sick." (Bernard Nathanson's organization, which became the first and largest abortion clinic in the Western World, was named the Center for Reproductive and Sexual *Health*.) And finally, "The Charitable Foundation for Institutional Care" was charged with the responsibility of collecting money from relatives for the cost of the killings of their loved ones—family members were never told what such charges were for (5:63).

The Nuremberg War Crime Trials ended less than a generation ago—well within the lifetime of most people now living. But it appears that the process of dehumanizing of life has begun all over again.

In America today, the medical profession is at the forefront of depersonalizing unborn children and calling them objects "in the way." They then proceed in the murdering of our unborn children under such euphemistically entitled practices as "Retrospective Fertility Control." Where will it end? How can the very people who obviously enjoy life and are so concerned over its "quality" so callously advocate the destruction of another's life merely because it is not their own or is somehow inconvenient? One wonders, would they have the same view if the tables were turned? In fact, modern America has more parallels to Nazi Germany than most are aware. In Pre-War Germany:

> The killing started with abortion in the very difficult cases, which then gradually extended to abortion-on-demand. When abortion became widespread, persons whose lives were considered "devoid of value" were killed.

> First to go were handicapped infants and children, then the mentally ill, then the terminally ill. Voluntary euthanasia (so called mercy killing) was next followed by involuntary euthanasia.

> With moral absolutes removed, the standard in Germany became a social and utilitarian one—the welfare of the state.

Classifying anyone as not worthy to live destroyed the absolute right of everyone. Upwards of 275,000 Aryan German men, women and children were sacrificed for the so-called 'social good' during the years prior to the Jewish Holocaust. Based on the philosophic and social trends, the Jewish Holocaust was the next logical step.

These same trends of the 1920's and 30's in Germany are gaining momentum in America today. Much of our own medical community and many groups in society are accepting death as an answer to medical and social dilemmas. Abortion-on-demand is legal. Reports of infants being allowed to die after birth, infanticide, are increasing. Suicide is encouraged through manuals that outline methods of "relieving suffering." Legislation advocating euthanasia is being proposed and even passed in state legislatures and is being promoted as acceptable through movies and the media in general. The first step being the "Living Will," followed by "Death with Dignity" legislation.

The obvious problem with such a trend is that once life is devalued, it is very difficult to draw the line. All human worth is placed in jeopardy. (47)

Given the extent and nature of the American abortion holocaust (26 million dead), are we hypocritical in condemning what Nazi Germany did? When literally billions of dollars are spent to destroy human life — legally, efficiently, cruelly and callously, are we headed for judgment just as surely as Germany?

We cannot dehumanize other persons without becoming less human ourselves:

> We cannot destroy life. We cannot regard the hydrocephalic child as a non-person and accept the responsibility for disposing of it like a sick animal. If there are those in society who think this step [destroying the severely deformed] would be good, . . . let them work for a totalitarian form of government where beginning with the infirm and incompetent and ending with the intellectually dissident, non-persons are disposed of day and night by those in power. (5:49-50)

If we are prepared to kill a child merely because it is handicapped, we are back in Hitler's Third Reich no matter how "noble" we consider our endeavors. Although abortions are promoted by those who consider themselves great humanitarians attempting to alleviate the suffering of others, the fact is, those of us who are "normal" are not better or greater than those who have mental or physical disabilities. The handicapped are simply differently gifted. The deformed and handicapped are not our problem — we are *their* problem. They do not wish to harm us; it is we who wish to destroy them.

The Scripture teaches that "God sees not as man sees, for man looks at the outward appearance, but the Lord looks at the heart" (I Sam. 16:7). Is there anyone who would say that the crippled and deformed are without a heart for God to observe?

Jesus went out of His way to care for the crippled and destitute: "And great multitudes came to Him, bringing with them those who were lame, crippled, blind, dumb, and many others, and they laid them down at His feet; and He healed them, so that the multitude marveled as they saw the dumb speaking, the crippled restored, and the lame walking, and the blind seeing; and they glorified the God of Israel" (Mt. 15:30-31). Jesus Himself said that even for our social engagements we were to "invite . . . the poor, the crippled, the lame, the blind, and you will be blessed, since they do not have the means to repay you" (Luke 14:13).

How often we hear of the special blessings that come to those parents with deformed children. What right does society have to take such special blessings either from the parents or the children: "Could it be that God has surprises hidden in those who are unlike us? Could it be that He intends them to stretch our narrow spirits, to help us grow in compassion and to teach us tolerance? Are the differences we judge to be strange, in reality simply 'special'? Is destruction of such life the best our society can offer?" (2:82).

Consider the testimony of Elaine Duckett, Glynn Verdon and Caryl Hodges, all of whom are severely disabled. Elaine has two useless arms and hands; Glynn, two useless legs, and Caryl has neither the use of arms nor legs. These disabled persons wrote a letter to the *London Daily Telegraph* when abortion was being suggested as a solution to the thalidomide problem. The drug thalidomide was responsible for many children being born deformed and handicapped just like these three ladies. In their letter they said:

> We were fortunate . . . in having been allowed to live and we want to say with strong conviction how thankful we are that none took it upon themselves to destroy us as helpless cripples. . . . We have found worthwhile and happy lives and we face our future with confidence. Despite our disability, life still has much to offer and we are more than anxious, if only metaphorically, to reach out toward the future. This, we hope, will give hope to the parents of the thalidomide babies, and at the same time serve to condemn those who would contemplate the destruction of even a limbless baby. (20:156-157)

In conclusion, the vast majority of handicapped people are grateful to be alive; they want to live. It only takes a little understanding to realize this would also have been true for those already aborted.

Questions for Discussion

1. Does the possibility of deformity justify an abortion? Explain.

2. Who should define what a "social handicap" is? Who should define what is valuable in terms of a human life?

3. Have you or do you know of anyone that has a deformed child or a child as a result of rape? If so, can you agree with Dr. Koop who says, "Many families

were better families than they would have been without the necessity of facing the adversity produced by the problems of the imperfect child"?

4. How is the modern attitude of abortions for convenience similar to attitudes current in Nazi Germany? On what basis can we be assured America will not travel a similar path?

5. How do infanticide, euthanasia and legally assisted suicide relate to abortion?

6. If we know that handicapped people are grateful to be alive, can we justify aborting deformed pre-borns? Is the same argument valid for all pre-borns?

7. Is it possible that "murder of the unborn" will establish precedents for eliminating other "dependents"? Explain your answer.

8. What does the Bible say about the crippled, innocent and the helpless?

WON'T RECRIMINALIZATION OF ABORTION INCREASE ILLEGAL ABORTIONS AND FORCE WOMEN INTO DANGEROUS "BACK ALLEY" OPERATIONS?

P rior to the legalization of abortion in 1973, the number of deaths from illegal abortions was apparently quite small — at most several hundred deaths per year (87;9:283-285).

But since the legalization of abortion, many *thousands* of women have died and many *millions* of babies have been killed. If legal abortions have increased, and if the abortion mortality rate is directly related to the inherent dangers of the abortion procedure, then it is reasonable to assume maternal deaths from abortion have also increased.

The abortion lobby has maintained that abortion is a safer procedure than childbirth, but this is false. The maternal death rate from childbirth is roughly .01 percent or 1 in 10,000; therefore, it is one of the safest of medical procedures. The maternal death rate from abortion is at least twice this and possibly as high as 20 times this figure (l:909-913, cf. 11:84-91). Thus, for the average healthy woman, "abortion is far more risky than childbirth" (9:113). But regardless, the child mortality rate from abortion is 100 percent — it is the most fatal surgical procedure in existence. Even saving hundreds of women cannot justify killing millions of babies (72:140).

Below we present six reasons why those who argue that abortion saves lives are wrong.

First, the abortion lobby has been unfair, even dishonest in its use of figures regarding the maternal death rates from abortion. For example, they repeatedly claimed a figure of 5,000-10,000 deaths per year from illegal abortions prior to *Roe v. Wade*. But these figures were apparently a political tool.

For example, in 1967 the Federal government reported 160 deaths from abortion; in 1972, only 39 deaths (9:283). Even with significant underreporting, the figures are nowhere near 5000-10,000 deaths a year. Consider the words of Dr. Bernard Nathanson, Co-founder of N.A.R.A.L.[National Abortion Rights Action League], director of New York's Center for Reproductive and Sexual Health (the largest abortion clinic in the Western World in the early 1970's), but now an outspoken opponent of abortion:

> How many deaths were we talking about when abortion was illegal? In N.A.R.A.L. we generally emphasized the drama of the individual case, not the mass statistics; but when we spoke of the latter it was always "5,000 to 10,000 deaths a year." I confess that I knew the figures were totally false, and I suppose the others did too if they stopped to think of it. But in the "morality" of our revolution, it was a useful figure, widely accepted, so why go out of our way to correct it with honest statistics? The overriding concern was to get the laws eliminated, and anything within reason that had to be done was permissible. (9:282; 72)

Second, the issue of "legal vs. illegal" abortion should not be our only concern.

Unfortunately, every horror that was true of illegal abortion is also true about legalized abortion. Many veterans of illegal abortion, however, do not realize this. Instead, they cling to the belief that all the pain and problems they suffered could have been avoided if only abortion had been legal. They imagine that if their abortions had been legal, their lives would somehow be better today. Instead of recognizing that it is the very nature of abortion itself which caused their problems, they blame their suffering on the illegality of abortion at that time. This is superficial blame shifting, but it is an understandable reaction to what is always a traumatic experience. (9:301)

Third, it is not necessarily true that legalization of abortion prevents criminal abortions. Illegal abortions continue to occur even in this country (8:215). Speaking before the 93rd Congress, Senator James L. Buckley stated:

Data from foreign countries having far longer experience with legalized abortion than we have had in the U.S. suggest that legalization has no effect on the criminal abortion rate. In at least three countries the criminal abortion rate has actually risen since legalization. Legalized abortion moves the back alley abortionists into the front office where their trade can be practiced without fear of criminal prosecution. (8:215)

In the minds of many women, it was the legalization of abortion that legitimized abortion as a genuine option. If abortion is once again criminalized, the vast majority of women will, once again, choose not to have an abortion. The argument that for every woman now having a legal abortion, seven would resort to illegal abortion is simply false (9:287-295).

Once there is a renewed restriction on abortion, the rate of illegal abortions would return to approximately pre-1973 levels. . . . There can be no doubt that laws against abortion would be effective in discouraging women from seeking abortions. Studies in foreign countries have shown that 40 to 85 percent of aborting women would not have aborted if it had been illegal. In our own survey of aborted women, over 90 percent said they would not have sought an illegal abortion or attempted self-abortion if the laws had been different. Nearly the same percentage reported that permissive abortion law strongly influenced their view of the morality of abortion.

If abortion was again totally restricted in the United States, it is likely that the rate of illegal abortions would again decline to around 100,000 to 200,000 per year, representing the demand of 'hard-core' aborters. . . . the complication and death rates would be much lower. . . . Even such leading abortion proponents as Garrett Hardin admit that recriminalization would not result in increased deaths or complications. (9:321-322)

Fourth, making abortion legal has proportionately increased the suffering and death of women, not decreased it:

According to the *reported* data, the number of deaths resulting from induced abortions, legal and illegal combined, has not dropped at all since 1973. "While maternal deaths due to criminal abortion appear to be decreasing, *they have been replaced, almost one for one, by maternal deaths due to legal abortion.*" [italics in original] Furthermore, although illegal abortions have been reduced, they continue to occur at a rate of approximately 15,000 per year . . . one isolated study . . . found . . . there were three times more abortion-related deaths *after* legalization.

In the simplest of terms . . . *the percentage chance of survival is improved, but the absolute number of those who suffer has increased!*

This is true not only in terms of abortion mortality, but also in terms of abortion complications. In 1969 the number of abortion-related complications which were treated in U.S. hospitals stood at 9,000. By 1977 the number of *reported* cases treated in hospitals had risen to 17,000. The total of all reported complications in 1977 was 100,000. . . . Again it should be remembered that these are the minimum, *reported* figures. . . . On top of the increased physical suffering must be added the deaths which are *indirectly* caused by abortion. Pro-abortionists may dismiss the deaths of tens of millions of "unwanted" children who are the intentional victims of abortion, but each year approximately 100,000 "wanted" pregnancies will end in sorrow of a spontaneous miscarriage because of latent abortion morbidity. . . . Rather than 100,000 or 200,000 illegal aborters facing the emotional trauma of abortion, now 1.5 million women each year are exposed to the psychological sequelae of abortion. . . .They will face a nine-fold tendency towards suicide. They will experience increased marital stress and broken relationships. They will be more and more driven to the escapist and self-punishing abuse of drugs and alcohol. They will be more prone to child battery, and many of their children will face the psychological burden of knowing that mother "killed" their brother or sister.

Is the marginal reduction of illegal abortions worth such a price? (9:291-293)

Fifth, abortion deaths are, in all likelihood significantly underreported: "It is quite possible that only 5 to 10 percent of all deaths resulting from legal abortion are being reported as abortion-related" (9:110).

Sixth, no law is observed 100 percent of the time; its value lies in its deterrent effect. Any reasonable law will not force people to break it. Preventing the killing of unborn human beings is a reasonable law. Criminalizing abortion will not result in "forcing" women into illegal abortions. To say illegality forces women to have an abortion simply denies their choice in the matter. Legal or illegal, no one is forced: the only difference is one of perception and legal culpability.

Further, "If people willfully break a law and hurt themselves in the process, their injuries are due to their irresponsible, illegal behavior. Repealing a law on the basis of the consequences one endures by willfully breaking that law is asinine" (75:15). Further, the argument today is largely irrelevant. Dr. Nathanson observes:

I mean, the coat hanger is an antiquated, an obsolete symbol. If in fact abortion were proscribed tomorrow morning, there's no question that women would resort to the new abortion pills. They would be smuggled into this country in great quantities and women would be using them. There would be no deaths from abortion; no coat hangers; no back-alleys. All of this is 1960's sloganeering. It has no place in the discussion in 1990. (87)

Questions for Discussion

1. Won't prohibition of abortion force women into dangerous "back alley" operations?

2. Has the abortion lobby been accurate in its use of figures concerning deaths from illegal abortions?

3. Are legal abortions fundamentally less horrible or consequential than illegal abortions?

4. Does legalization of abortion necessarily affect the criminal abortion rate?

5. How does legalization of abortion relate to the morality of abortion? Why is it important that abortion be illegal?

6. Does abortion save lives?

7. Has the legalizing of abortion increased the suffering and death of women? Give examples.

8. Why do you think abortion deaths are underreported?

DON'T OPINION POLLS FAVOR ABORTION?

B ecause the outcome is so important to each side, both parties in the abortion debate seek to bolster their views by
showing that the clear majority of Americans agree with them.
But before we proceed further, we should observe that whoever
uses this argument to justify their position engages in a logical
fallacy known as "appeal to the majority." Majority opinion may
or may not be right; an issue must be decided on its own merits,
not popular opinion. "The majority" have been wrong in the
past — and with disastrous consequences. When it comes to abortion, millions of Americans are inadequately informed.

Why do both sides claim the majority supports their position? The reasons are complex, but usually result from poor
methods of polling, biased interpretations of data, margin of
error, certain inherent problems in surveying public beliefs and
the wording of questions. For example, a 1982 Gallup poll
showed 77 percent agreed that an abortion should be decided
solely by a woman and her physician (*New York Times,* Jan. 22,
1982). But another Gallup poll a few months later showed only
24 percent agreed that a woman should have an abortion without
her husband's consent (49). Thus:

On sensitive issues such as abortion, how questions are phrased may account for apparent shifts in public opinion as large as 28 percent. Two recent studies, for example, noted that simply reversing the order of items asked produced apparent shifts as large as 17 percent. . . .

If a question about abortion contains the phrase "terminate pregnancy" or "women's right to . . . " or the words "doctor, choice, the embryo, the fetus" the answer of the majority will be pro-abortion.

If the question uses the words "abortion for social or economic reasons" (which are 98 percent of them) or "the unborn or pre-born baby," "his or her" (rather than "its"), "abortionist," "choice to kill," or "civil or human right of the unborn baby," the answer of the majority will be pro-life. (49)

Pollsters have long known that the outcome of a poll can be manipulated by how the question is phrased. For example, notice how the manner in which the question is put tends to elicit the response desired:

A. Should a Woman Be Granted the Choice of an Abortion?

This question is too general. The reader must answer yes or no to a question that incorporates an assumption most already hold (the right of choice over no choice) but without a proper evaluation of the issue. Certainly all readers will not answer this question the same way if additional information is supplied. Do they believe a woman should be granted an abortion at 8-1/2 months? In fact, when asked if they think a woman should be granted an abortion merely to suit her personal whims, convenience or lifestyle, 77 percent of Americans say, "No." (See "C" below.)

B. Should a Raped Woman Be Forced to Carry a Child to Term?

The word *forced* has negative connotations and almost demands a negative answer. But no one is speaking of forcing anyone; this question centers upon the issue of coercion, not the nature and rights of the pre-born and the option of adoption. The proper question we should address is whether society should assume the innocent child has no rights in cases of rape. How would people answer the following question: Should the rights of the child be considered in rape?

In addition, the overall relevancy of this question is rarely stated, that is, people are not told that only .06 percent of abortions arise from rape. Further, a "No" answer to this question may be wrongly interpreted by pollsters as a consensus for abortion in general.

C. Do You Believe the Government Should Require Poor Women to Assume the Burden of Another Child?

Again, the center of attention is on the woman, subjective perception ("burden") and coercion, not the child; a more important issue is obscured. What about the woman's responsibility for getting pregnant? What about the father's responsibility to support? What about adoption? What if the woman wants to keep her child and society can help pay the expenses? All these issues are ignored.

In conclusion, in order for a poll to *accurately* reflect the views of the country on abortion, it must ask fair and precise questions which accurately reflect the complexity of the problem. When this is done, the facts are clear: ". . . public opinion predominantly favors strong restrictions against abortion. Indeed, polls show strong public support, 71 to 76 percent, in

favor of some form of state or local regulation of abortion"
(9:312).

According to David C. Reardon:

> Most polls agree with this general breakdown: about 20 per-
> cent of all people reject abortion under any circumstances, 20
> to 25 percent would leave it solely to the woman's choice, and
> the majority, 55 to 60 percent, would limit abortion to specific
> circumstances, particularly the "hard" cases. (9:311-312)

Thus, Americans are not in favor of abortion as it is practiced in this country: abortion on demand. They are in favor of
abortion in the "hard cases"—the 2 to 5 percent involving rape,
incest, the mother's life, certain kinds of deformity, etc. According to James A. Davis, *General Social Surveys, 1972-1985* (Chicago: National Opinion Research Center, 1985), which
incorporates careful analysis of 14 years of surveys and other
research, the abortion industry is not correct in its claims.

> Approximately 98 percent of all abortions are performed for
> social, non-medical reasons, but 77 percent of the American
> public opposes permitting abortion for these reasons.
>
> The majority oppose abortion in nearly all circumstances or
> oppose it with the exception for certain 'hard cases' such as
> danger to the mother's health, rape, incest or the possibility of
> serious handicap in the child. . . .
>
> Support for legalized abortion drops significantly when re-
> spondents are asked to consider abortion after the first three
> months of pregnancy. There is no majority support for abor-
> tion under any circumstances after this point, except where
> the mother's life is in danger. . . .
>
> Support for legalized abortion also drops sharply when re-
> spondents are asked to consider specific circumstances such
> as the husband's role in the abortion decision and abortion
> because of the child's sex instead of vague generalities. (cited
> in ref. 49)

An article in *Family Planning Perspectives* (July/August, 1981, p. 163) revealed that even among N.A.R.A.L. (National Abortion Rights Action League) members, 85 percent were in favor of abortion for any reason, but only 58 percent supported legalized abortion when the child was not of the preferred sex (49). Still, the fact that almost 60 percent of these people might kill their children merely to have a different sex seems incredible!

Although the abortion lobby frequently claims that most women want the right to abortion, this too is false; far more women are against abortion:

> The pressure to regulate abortion is growing. And it is no wonder, because with each passing year the myths of abortion are increasingly exposed, particularly the myth that women want the "right" to abortion. In fact, the opposite is true: "virtually every poll shows that women are significantly more anti-abortion than men are."

> In terms of political activists, far more women are working against abortion than for it. In the nation's largest pro-life group, the National Right to Life Committee, there are 7.5 million women working to stop abortion and provide positive alternatives to women with unplanned pregnancies. In the nation's largest pro-choice organization, the National Abortion Rights Action League, there are only 121,000 female members. Even if one included all of the 250,000 members of the National Organization of Women, the largest feminist group which supports abortion, there are still over twenty women working against abortion for every one woman working for it. And as we saw in Chapter Two, women who have actually had abortions are six times more likely to become anti-abortion advocates than pro-choice activists. (9:312-313)

The fact that this many women do not want to have abortions proves that American society has failed a large part of its entire population (9:10). Here is one of the real tragedies of abortion—a society that will not help support a woman through childbirth and beyond, but which instead applies such pressures as to make abortion seem the only realistic option (9:10,30,32).

Finally, 65 percent of Americans believe abortion is *morally* wrong; 55 percent believe it should be *illegal* except in the "hard" cases, and in 1973, less than 15 percent agreed with the Supreme Court decision that human life begins at viability — 36 percent of men and 50 percent of women believed it began at conception (49). Almost 10 years later, a Gallup poll revealed that 54 percent of the respondents believed life began at conception and only 18 percent agreed with the Court that minors may obtain abortions without parental consent (49).

The conclusion is that no one should trust an opinion poll unless they know enough about it to justify their trust. Abortion policy today reveals we do not have *true* public policy; we have *private policy:* laws established by un-elected justices who gave in to a decade of pressure from a minority of social engineers who decided to impose their beliefs on the rest of society. And the Supreme Court continues to support them. *Roe v. Wade* and *Doe v. Bolton* in 1973 were only the first two of 16 subsequent Supreme Court decisions upholding abortion (49; 25:41-43). Since the *Webster* decision in 1989, the Court's direction may be changing; but this cannot excuse almost twenty years of decisions that were morally, scientifically, legally and sociologically bankrupt.

Questions for Discussion

1. What is an "appeal to the majority"?

2. What part does language play in the results of an opinion poll? Give two illustrations.

3. What does research show about the percentage of the American public who opposed permitting abortion? Give details.

IS ABORTION AN ENTIRELY SAFE MEDICAL PROCEDURE?

E arlier we saw that abortion is not "an entirely safe medical procedure" for either the mother or society, to say nothing of the pre-born child. This argument is simply another ruse of the abortion promoters. But this does not stop abortion propagandists from continuing to deceive the public.

Questions for Discussion

1. Discuss again the physical results for women who have abortions.

2. Name some of the psychological results for women who have abortions.

AREN'T THERE TOO MANY PEOPLE IN THE WORLD?

The population explosion is a myth. For example, from 1975 to 1989 the world's population has grown less than 1.8 percent. In fact, 4.5 billion people, the world's population, could be placed in the state of Texas in one gigantic city with the population density less than that of many existing cities, leaving the rest of the globe completely empty (75:1). (The problem is not too many people as much as it is the distribution of resources.)

Questions for Discussion

1. Do you agree that there are too many people in the world?

2. If so, what do you think should be done about it?

Question 29

ISN'T THE IDEA THAT HUMAN LIFE BEGINS AT CONCEPTION MERELY A RELIGIOUS BELIEF OF SOME PEOPLE?

A s we have documented, the life of a human being begins at conception—this is a scientific fact, not a religious belief—and to believe otherwise ignores biological reality. Further, only biological criteria may be used to define a human being because whenever non-biological criteria are used, in principle anyone can be defined as non-human. Not a single term is ever used to describe the unborn—zygote, morula, blastocyst, embryo or fetus—which means "not living." That which resides in the woman's womb possessing its own body, genetic code, metabolism and destiny which is growing, developing and thriving must be alive. If a pre-born's life was not as biologically definitive as any other human being's, then killing it would not be necessary for its removal (75:2-3).

The position of religious faith is on the part of the pro-choice individual, not the pro-life individual. To deny the preborn is a human being is biological nonsense; it is not religion that determines the fact of when a human being physically exists; it is science. The "pro-choice" view that the fetus is not human, not a human individual, is the philosophical (religious) tenet which is completely out of harmony with scientifically verifiable fact. Finally, the arguments against abortion are not only biological and medical, they are also psychological, social, legal, demographic and ethical. Religion per se need not even enter the picture (101:ix).

Questions for Discussion

1. Isn't the idea that life begins at conception a religious belief? Or is it a scientific fact?

2. Does religion even enter the picture? Give facts to prove your answer.

IF ABORTION IS CRIMINALIZED, WON'T WOMEN GO TO JAIL? AREN'T PRO-LIFE PEOPLE TRYING TO PUNISH WOMEN?

P ro-life people aren't trying to punish women but to save the lives of true human children. Here we must distinguish between women who have an abortion in ignorance of the facts and those who knowingly take another's life. Why should not both men and women who knowingly take the life of their own child be subject to some form of punishment? Men and women who are ignorant of the facts, or have been the victims of the lies of others, should not be punished.

Why are many women victims even though they freely choose to have an abortion? It is because they are typically insufficiently informed as to the nature of the fetus and the dangers of the abortion process. Further, in the same manner that a drug addict is termed a victim of drugs, and one who takes his life is commonly called a suicide victim, the mother who aborts her child is an abortion victim (75:11). If anyone deserves punishment, it is the doctors who perform abortions. Though the mother may indeed be a victim, every physician who performs abortions knows more than enough concerning human life to be guilty.

Questions for Discussion

1. Will women be unfairly victimized if abortion is criminalized?

2. If abortion is criminalized, what effect would this have on doctors who perform abortions?

WHAT ABOUT BIRTH CONTROL PILLS?

The word "contraceptive" is being misused by some people today. They use this word in referring to drugs that really end a pregnancy by destroying the already developing human. But a *true* contraceptive should do no more than *prevent* the sperm and egg from uniting to form a zygote, i.e., a human life.

Are Birth Control Pills Abortifacients?

On the other hand, some people have wrongly claimed that *all* birth control pills are abortifacients.* But we do not think it accurate to label all birth control pills as abortifacients. However, we hasten to add that we accept the right of any person to disagree with us as a matter of conscience.

---

* We agree that some certainly are. For example, the European pill RU-486 is strictly an abortion pill. Why? The only function of this pill is to bring about a woman's menstrual flow, thus expelling the already fertilized egg. We discuss other strictly abortifacient pills later in this question. Besides pills, another abortifacient is the IUD which prevents the already developing embryo from implanting in the uterus.

Here is the specific data on how birth control pills work and why we do not think they are abortifacients.

First, birth control pills act primarily to prevent ovulation. This is their main function. If ovulation does not occur, there will be no egg released that may be fertilized by the sperm. No human can be conceived and no pregnancy occurs. Birth control pills are 98-99 percent effective in stopping the egg from being released.

In addition to this primary function, there are also secondary effects from the Pill. The hormone progestin in the pill causes the mucous at the cervix, the opening to the womb, to become very gelatinous, thick, and hence impenetrable to the sperm. As a result, even if there were an egg released, it would be much harder for the sperm to get through the mucous barrier at the cervix and continue into the uterus and up the Fallopian tube to fertilize the egg.

Birth control pills also cause a change in the endometrium, the lining of the uterus, so that it may become inhospitable or uninhabitable for a fertilized egg. Because of this effect, if an egg comes down the Fallopian tube and has been fertilized, it is believed that it cannot implant in the uterine wall. Instead, it would be expelled in an abortive manner.

This last effect is why pharmaceutical manufacturers always add an addendum that birth control pills "may" prevent implantation. But doctors admit that if cases do occur, the number is so minutely small that it is almost nonexistent.

Further, concerning the possibility that birth control pills affect the lining of the uterus, it is a known fact that some women do get pregnant even though they have taken the Pill regularly. This tends to show that even in rare cases when an egg has been fertilized, there is no abortion effect.

How effective is the Pill? Pharmaceutical manufacturers estimate that hindrance of ovulation, that is, preventing the egg from emerging, fails less than two percent of the time or is 98-

99 percent effective. Including all three effects of the Pill, statistics show that women who regularly take birth control pills have a failure rate of only one tenth of one percent.

Theoretically, if ovulation occurs and if the sperm is somehow able to penetrate the mucous at the cervix, possibly the lining of the uterus *may* then be inhospitable to the fertilized egg and thus act as an abortifacient. For those who because of conscience would not want to risk this, we must respect their choice.

But given the *theoretical* possibility that the Pill might cause an abortion (however rare), does this mean that women who are concerned over this should never use the Pill? We believe the answer is *no*.

We would like to thank Bob Christmas, M.D., for the following illustrations that put this matter into proper perspective. He uses as examples three common practices: driving a car, performing non-emergency surgery, and taking birth control pills.

He reasons that most people travel by car even though there is a slight chance that they will hit and kill another human being. They have no intent of killing anyone. Yet even though there is a slight chance it could happen, they still drive. Should people refuse to drive cars in order to avoid any chance of causing a traffic death? No.

Physicians routinely do surgery even though they know there is a slight chance that every time they operate, the patient may die. Should physicians never operate because of the rare chance the patient will die? No.

When it comes to birth control pills, the issue is similar. Should someone refuse to take birth control pills if there is the slightest chance a child may die? No one can demonstrate an abortion has ever occurred by using birth control pills; and clearly the intent of the user is far different from one who takes a "morning after" pill specifically designed to cause an abortion.

In conclusion, since the primary intent and goal of birth control pills is to prevent the sperm and the egg from meeting, and there is no sure evidence that the birth control pill acts to expel the fertilized egg, we conclude that birth control pills are not abortifacients.

What Are the Implications of RU-486 and Related Compounds?

RU-486 (Mifepristone), WIN-3279, Epostane, Trilostane ZK-98-299 (Onapristone), ZK-98-734 (Lilopristone) and similar largely experimental compounds are drugs designed to destroy the unborn very early in pregnancy. Many more are in various stages of production (51:7).

Given the tremendous funds and effort exerted on behalf of these compounds, not to mention the holocaust itself, an alien visiting this planet might just conclude the earthlings believed (of all things!) that pregnancy itself was a disease and that earthmen were half-bent on self-destruction. Situation ethicist Joseph Fletcher has even stated that an "unwanted" pregnancy "is a disease — in fact a venereal disease" (7:58).

In effect these compounds are extremely lucrative drugs which make abortion much less messy, perhaps safer and much more private. For example, when given with prostaglandin, RU-486 becomes a 100 percent effective abortefacient (1:165).

> In general these drugs are most effective in producing abortion if administered within the first seven weeks of the pregnancy. RU-486 was disappointing . . . it would cause a pregnancy to die through its anti-progesterone effect, it was not uniformly successful in expelling the dead unborn child: women given this drug would continue to bleed and would require either the administration of other drugs such as prostaglandins (Gemeprost) or a suction D. and C. to remove the dead pregnancy.

However, the investigators of ZK-98-734 claim that this latest weapon not only kills the pregnancy, but also acts to expel it quickly with no need for prostaglandins and/or suction D. and C. More chilling is their finding that if the drug is given very early in the pregnancy (3-4 weeks), the entire pregnancy will be resorbed, i.e. it will simply disappear, leaving no trace; there is no bleeding, no expulsion of tissue, nothing to identify this as an abortion. (51:7)

The current status and distribution of these compounds, at least in America, is uncertain. (They are currently used in France, China, and other countries.) However, the abortion industry is using the full weight of its lobbying ability to make these compounds widely available throughout the world (31). Although these drugs kill a human being just as surely as any other induced abortion, the pressure is on to defuse and sanitize the process of chemical abortion. Thus, some refer to them as only "menstrual inducers."

We must remember that these compounds still destroy a human being, a person. The person is destroyed at only a slightly younger age than abortions which are routinely performed at a later stage. This is why those who care about the unborn must organize effectively and oppose the production of these compounds. Widely used, they would only accelerate our national rush to self-destruction:

We are seeing now only the leading edge of the technology of pharmacologic abortion. Doubtless, other more sophisticated, more deadly drugs will appear from other manufacturers. . . . The pressure to release these drugs to market may become too great, and boycotts will fail (it is also conceivable that virtually every major drug manufacturer in the U.S. will have its own name-brand abortifacient on the shelf, and we could find ourselves boycotting twenty or thirty different companies simultaneously — hardly practical). . . .

The most effective counter to this pervasive biologic warfare is (a) to insist on rigid (by the book) testing of each of these drugs, a process which given the complex nature and action of these drugs might consume years, and (b) launch a major educational effort to school the public to the potential long-term hazards of these drugs, citing the DES and thalidomide experiences and (c) persuading the nation that abortion — like smoking and alcohol — is bad for your health (to say nothing of your unborn child's health). (51:8)

Questions for Discussion

1. Are all birth control pills abortifacients? Why?

2. What is the problem with "contraceptives" that destroy the zygote?

3. What are RU-486 and related compounds?

4. What church strategy can you think of to help prevent abortion pills from becoming widely available?

WON'T THE CRIMINALIZATION OF ABORTION CAUSE THE POOR TO SUFFER WHILE THE RICH WILL SIMPLY CONTINUE TO GET ABORTIONS?

The question is: Is abortion good or evil? Restricting something evil does not cause suffering to those who can no longer secure it. In fact, it is the rich who will suffer because their children will be killed. If the availability of hard drugs were greatly restricted so that prices increased a hundredfold, and only the rich could afford them, would we argue that the poor were being discriminated against? No. The poor would be spared the consequences of drug abuse while the rich would suffer (75:14).

Questions for Discussion

1. Does poverty or wealth justify abortion?

2. Does restricting something that is evil favor either the rich or the poor? Give illustrations to prove your point.

SHOULDN'T ABORTION BE RESTRICTED ONLY AFTER VIABILITY?

E ventually, new technology will push back the time babies are viable to the time of conception. Since *Roe v. Wade*, the time of legally perceived viability has already been reduced from 28 weeks to 19 weeks.

Further, is even a newborn infant truly viable? The fact is that for several years newborn infants are dependent upon their mothers for their very lives. They are biologically viable but not autonomously viable. And they are not even biologically viable for very long. Further, "If anything, non-viability is a compelling reason against abortion, because a baby so young does not yet possess even a fighting chance to survive. Protection should be given to those who need it most" (75:16).

All human beings are nonviable outside the uterus for the first five months or so. What this argument really means is that "open season" exists on babies up until five months. "Thus, a murderous time clock is established: 'Kill your baby now, before it's too late'" (75:16a).

Questions for Discussion

1. What problem does technology present to viability?

2. In what sense is even a two-year-old non-viable?

3. How does viability promote abortion?

WHO IS GOING TO DECIDE THAT AN ABORTION MAY OR MAY NOT OCCUR – THE INDIVIDUAL OR THE STATE?

The real question is not who should make the choice but whether the choice should be made in the first place. Killing pre-born infants should not be a choice at all. No one should have the right, whether an individual or the state. The death of an innocent child should always be the result of natural causes and not of direct human intervention with destructive intent (75:17).

Were the issue one of murder, robbery, slavery or rape the question would not even be considered (75:17). Who is going to decide to do such things, the individual or the state? Before the Civil War slave masters were adamantly "pro-choice" concerning their right to slavery. They were so convinced that this choice belonged to them and not the government that they caused one of the most catastrophic wars in American history.

Questions for Discussion

1. Who is going to decide that an abortion may or may not occur? Should the individual or the state?

2. What might be some of the consequences of letting the state decide such questions as who is going to live and who isn't?

3. Is it right to think that you can disobey a law because you have a "right" to choose for yourself?

IF TODAY THE STATE CAN PROHIBIT ABORTION, WHO IS TO SAY THE STATE WILL NOT DECIDE TO FORCE ABORTION IN THE FUTURE, AS IS DONE IN CHINA?

What a strange line of reasoning that asserts a positive evil must now be continued, because a future evil may result.

> Such an argument neglects to examine why legal abortion should be restricted. Calls for proscription (condemnation) are based upon the humanity of the pre-born child, the inalienable right to life our Constitution guarantees, and the primary purpose of a government to protect its people. The objective is not merely to restrict women's "choices," just as abolishing slavery was not sought merely to restrict whites' "choices." In both cases, a higher, nobler objective is espoused. (75:18)

Further, once abortion is declared illegal, the state would never force abortions on women. Only changes of unimaginable proportions could bring this about. And such unimaginable changes should not be the basis for deciding policy today.

Questions for Discussion

1. On what basis should we decide public policy on abortion: current reality or hypothetical possibility? Explain.

2. What is meant by "the inalienable right to life" guaranteed by out constitution? How does this apply to the abortion issue?

ISN'T IT TRUE THAT PRO-ABORTION IS FORCED ABORTION WHERE PRO-CHOICE IS ONLY FOR THE RIGHT TO CHOOSE?

P ro-choice is a euphemism for pro-abortion. The only issue is abortion, and if the choice is for abortion, the position is synonymous with pro-abortion. One cannot separate the choice from its object. For example, to say, "We are not in favor of rape, only for the right to choose whether or not to do it," is no different than being for rape.

Further, pro-choice groups can hardly be described as neutral observers; their actions belie them as pro-abortion. "In reality, with the pressures women face against giving birth, the pro-abortion concealment of facts, and the one-sided 'counseling' abortuaries provide, a 'forced choice' is what most of today's abortions really are" (75:20b).

Questions for Discussion

1. Explain why the argument "I'm pro-choice not pro-abortion" is invalid.

2. Are pro-choice advocates biased in their own viewpoint?

IS ABORTION THE MOST COR-
RECT AND MORAL DECISION
FOR A WOMAN WHO HAS
ALREADY HAD TWO OR
MORE CHILDREN?

Subjective feelings must be defended. Why was abortion better—more moral, more right, than adoption? Why for you and why for your child? Aren't we really dealing here with selfish motives? (75:21).

The bottom line for abortion is based in our individual and national self-centeredness. Many people want the freedom to abort merely to cover the consequences of their own sexual immorality. One sin covers another; murder becomes the "solution" to fornication or adultery. One evil justifies another. But when one's lifestyle dictates one's moral philosophy, we are headed toward anarchy.

Consider drug abuse. A minority of people today think it is right to disobey the law, feeling they have the "right" to use a variety of drugs for their own personal pleasure. Yet anyone familiar with the personal, social and international consequences of drug abuse will find it impossible to decriminalize the use of drugs. Yet we have decriminalized abortion, homosexuality, gambling and other acts which should be criminalized for the welfare of society.

Billions of dollars and man hours are expended on the "war on drugs." The vast majority of Americans support a national effort to reduce drug abuse due to the increasingly visible effects of drug abuse around them. But how can we wage war on substance or child abuse and ignore the abuse of pre-born children? Maybe it is because the mass destruction is less obvious. If 26 million aborted fetuses were strewn across the land, openly displayed on our city streets, maybe that would change the minds of Americans.

To some degree the German population knew of the Jewish holocaust and did nothing. America bears more guilt: all of us know 1.5 to 2 million babies are slaughtered each year.*

Questions for Discussion

1. Can subjective feelings alone justify any belief?

2. Does number of children justify abortion?

3. Should lifestyle dictate moral philosophy?

4. Do you feel America has been guilty of murder by allowing abortion? Explain.

5. Can we be concerned about the war on drugs and logically neglect the war on the unborn?

---

* Note: the authors would like to acknowledge their indebtedness to Robert Evangelisto (75) and David Reardon (9) for portions of this material.

ABORTION: A BIBLICAL AND THEOLOGICAL ANALYSIS

INTRODUCTION

T his chapter is written specifically for Christians concerning what the Bible teaches on the subject of abortion and life in the womb. Why do we feel it is important to have a section just for Christians? If you are a Christian, you believe that the Bible is the Word of God. But what God says in the Bible isn't just human speculation or good advice—it is God's Word. When God says something is true, it *is* true and therefore we should believe it and act on it. That is why we are putting these Biblical verses in this section. We assume that if we document what the Bible teaches in this area, that it will not go in one ear and out the other but that it will help Christians to be better informed on this issue.

For those who are not Christians, you may wonder, why do we accept that what the Bible teaches is accurate and relevant to the question of abortion? Put simply, because the historical evidence compels us to. Let us briefly cite a few reasons for our beliefs.

First, the science of textual criticism has proven beyond doubt that we have an accurate text of the original Bible and that it has not been corrupted over the centuries. For example, studies of the New Testament prove that it has been copied with over 99 percent accuracy and that the remaining 1 percent or less does not affect any significant teaching (110). The Old Testament has also been accurately transmitted (126).

Anyone who reads the New Testament accounts can see they involve eyewitness testimony (e.g., Luke 1:1-3; 1 John 1:1; 1 Corinthians 15:6-8). Yet in 2,000 years, no valid reason has ever been put forth which would cause us to doubt the accuracy or the integrity of the Biblical writers.

Second, because these writers accurately record the words of Jesus Christ, it is a historical fact that Jesus Christ lived and taught what the New Testament says He lived and taught. Jesus claimed to be God (John 5:18; 10:17-18, 27-33) and gave proof of this in His resurrection from the dead. His physical resurrection from the dead is an established historical fact. Indeed, if any fact of history is to be trusted, it is the resurrection of Jesus Christ from the dead (cf. 1 Corinthians 15:3-18). If Jesus rose from the dead, then His claims about Himself must be true. He must be God (Rom. 1:4). In 2,000 years, the critic of the resurrection has yet to prove his case (111).

The early Gospel writers were all eyewitnesses of the resurrection (1 Corinthians 15:3-8; John 20:19-29). They were not fools (Luke 1:1-3). Several were skeptics and all of them had to be convinced by direct appearances of the risen Jesus (John 20:25; Luke 24:21). Some even called the idea "nonsense" (Luke 24:11). But after seeing Christ repeatedly in many different circumstances over a period of forty days (Acts 1:3; Luke 24:1-53), after testing their own senses, they were convinced. For example, Luke was both a trained physician and a careful historical researcher (Acts 1:3; Luke 1:1-3). Even the classical scholar and outstanding archaeologist Sir William Ramsay said, "Luke's history is unsurpassed in respect of its trustworthiness" (125:81). An initial skeptic of the New Testament, his own detailed firsthand archaeological investigations proved to him that Luke was a historian of the first rank (125:3-422). Yet, it is this same Luke who speaks of "many convincing proofs" for the physical resurrection of Christ from the dead (Acts 1:3).

Third, Jesus Himself believed the entire Old Testament was the literal Word of God (Matthew 4:4; John 17:17). This can be established from reading what He said. Because Jesus was God, He is an infallible authority. In this role, He taught that Scripture originates from God and is inerrant. Therefore, His complete trust in the Old Testament authenticates it as God's Word (112).

Fourth, the Bible repeatedly claims to be the inspired Word of God (2 Timothy 3:16; 1 Thessalonians 2:13, etc.) and supplies many evidences for this (118). For example, the Bible contains dozens of instances of clear supernatural predictions of future events (e.g., Isaiah 9:6; 7:14; 39:5-7; 44:28-45:4; 53:4-11; Micah 5:2; 1 Kings 13:1-2). These cannot be explained away on the basis of rationalistic presuppositions or other skeptical grounds (113).

Fifth, both Jesus Christ and true Biblical Christianity are unique among the world's religions, prophets and teachings (115). No other religious leader claimed to be God and proved it by rising from the dead. No other religion teaches salvation is solely by God's grace. No other religion is so inextricably bound to historical facts. No other religious scripture is like the Bible. For example, Professor Ernst Wurthwein observes in his *The Text of the Old Testament,* "No book in the literature of the world has been so often copied, printed, translated, read, and studied as the Bible. It stands uniquely as the object of so much effort devoted to preserving it faithfully, to understanding it, and to making it understandable to others" (126:117).

Sixth, its influence among mankind is incalculable. Millions of lives have been radically changed by encountering the living Jesus Christ.

Seventh, a large number of scholars and even skeptics have been converted to faith on the basis of the historical evidence alone (117).

Eighth, some of the best defenses of the Christian faith ever produced have been penned by noted lawyers and legal scholars who are expertly trained in dealing with evidence (119).

For these reasons and more, we believe the Bible is trustworthy and what it teaches is worthy of being considered on the abortion issue.

But we need to realize that God did not speak in technical, scientific language. He spoke in everyday language that would be understandable to all people. This is the kind of language that God inspired through the prophets.

What God clearly said was that life in the womb at any stage is of equal value to adult human life. He did not tell us precisely how the soul is given to men (e.g., directly by Him or by physical procreation), nor did He tell us the specific point at which the soul is given.

But this does not mean that we may conclude the soul is not given at conception. Based on the data we will discuss, our conclusion is that because from conception the value of life is equal at every point and because at every point God teaches this life is of equal value with adult life, we must assume that the soul exists from the point of conception. Given the Biblical evidence, we cannot reasonably come to any other conclusion.

Questions for Discussion

1. Why is the Bible relevant to the issue of abortion today?

2. Give eight reasons why the Bible can be trusted.

Question 38

WHAT DOES THE BIBLE
TEACH ABOUT ABORTION?

W e shall present nine lines of Biblical argument showing
that abortion is morally wrong: (A) Scriptures which reveal that God views the fetus in the womb as a full human life, a
person; (B) Scriptures which teach that God relates to the unborn
in a personal manner; (C) Scriptures which indicate some men
are called to God's service or purpose from the womb; (D)
Scriptures which indicate that all human life belongs to God; (E)
Scriptures that teach we must defend and protect the weak, the
defenseless, the innocent, the needy and the unwanted; (F) Scriptures which indicate that God has a plan and purpose even for the
handicapped and deformed; (G) Scriptures which indicate that
the personhood of Christ was present from conception; (H)
Scriptures that speak of God giving man "a soul"; (I) and finally,
an analysis of the controversial passage Exodus 21:22-25.

A. Scriptures Which Reveal That God Views
the Fetus as a Person Prohibit Abortion

In the Old Testament, the Bible uses the same Hebrew words to
describe the pre-born, infants and children. In the New Testa-

ment, the same Greek words also describe the pre-born, infants and children which indicates a continuity from conception to childhood and on into adulthood.

Examples in the New Testament:

The Greek word *brephos* is often used of the newly-born, infants and older children (Luke 2:12, 16; 18:15; 1 Peter 2:2). For example, in Acts 7:19 *brephos* refers to the children killed at Pharaoh's command. But in Luke 1:41, 44 this same word is used of John the Baptist while he was yet a fetus in the womb, a pre-born infant.

In God's eyes he was indistinguishable from "a child." The Biblical writer also informs us that John was filled with the Holy Spirit while still in his mother's womb, indicating personhood (Luke 1:15). Even three months before birth, John could miraculously recognize Jesus in Mary's womb (Luke 1:44).

In addition, the Greek *huios* means "son" but is used in Luke 1:36 of John the Baptist's existence in the womb before birth at six months.

Examples in the Old Testament:

The Hebrew word *yeled* is usually used of children—i.e., a child, boy, etc. But in Exodus 21:22 it is used of a child in the womb. In Genesis 25:22 the word *yeladim* (children) is used of Rebecca's children struggling while in her womb. In Job 3:3 Job uses the word *geber* to describe his conception: "A man child is conceived." But *geber* is a Hebrew noun that is usually translated as man, male or husband. In Job 3:11-16, Job equates the pre-born child with kings, counselors and princes.

All these Scriptures and many others indicate that God does not make a distinction between potential life and real life, or in delineating stages of personhood; namely, between a pre-born infant in the womb at any stage and a born infant or child. The

Scripture repeatedly assumes the continuity of a person from conception to adulthood. In fact, no separate word is used exclusively of a fetus that will permit it to be distinguished from an infant as far as its personhood and value are concerned.

B. Scripture Which Teach That God Relates to the Unborn in a Personal Manner Prohibit Abortion

In Psalm 139:16 the Psalmist says concerning God, "Your eyes saw my unformed body." The writer used the word *golem*, translated as "body" or "substance," to describe himself while he was in the womb. He uses this term to refer to God's personal care for him even during the first part of the embryonic state (from implantation up to the first few weeks), the state before the fetus is physically "formed" into a miniature human being. We know that the embryo is "unformed" for only four or five weeks. In other words, even in the "unformed body" stage of gestation (0-4 weeks), God says that He is caring for and molding a child (Psalm 139:13-16).

Other Scriptures indicate that God relates to the fetus as a person. Job 31:15 says, "Did not He who *made me in the womb* make him? Did not the same one form us both within our mothers?"

In Job 10:8-11 we read, "Your hands *formed me and made me altogether*. . . . You have clothed me with skin and flesh, and have knit me together with bones and sinews."

Psalm 78:5-6 reveals God's concern over "the children yet to be born."

Psalm 139:13-16 states, "For you *created my inmost being;* you *knit me together* in my mother's womb. I praise you because I am fearfully and wonderfully made; . . . My frame was not hidden from you when I was made in the secret place. When I was woven together in the depths of the earth, your eyes saw my unformed body."

These Scriptures reveal that personal pronouns are used to describe the relationship between God and those in the womb.

In Genesis 25:22-24, the Bible says, "But the children struggled together within her; . . . And the Lord said to her, 'Two nations are in your womb; And two people shall be separated from your body; And one people shall be stronger than the other; And the older shall serve the younger.' When her days to be delivered were fulfilled, behold, there were twins in her womb." This shows that the two fetuses in Rebekah's womb were referred to as children before they were born.

C. Scriptures Which Indicate Some Men Are Called to God's Service or Purpose from the Womb Prohibit Abortion

There are many verses like those below which indicate that God views the pre-born in the womb as persons:

Jeremiah 1:5 — Before I formed you in the womb I knew you, before you were born I set you apart; I appointed you as a prophet to the nations.

Galatians 1:15-16 — But when He who set me apart, even from my mother's womb and called me through His grace, was pleased to reveal his Son in me, that I might preach Him among the Gentiles.

Judges 13:3, 5 — The angel of the Lord appeared to her and said, "You are sterile and childless, but you are going to conceive and have a son. . . . No razor may be used on his head, because the boy is a Nazirite, set apart to God from birth, and he will begin the deliverance of Israel from the hands of the Philistines."

Isaiah 49:1, 5 — Listen to Me, O islands, and pay attention, you peoples from afar. The Lord called Me from the womb; from the body of My mother He named Me. . . . And now says the Lord, who formed Me from the womb to be His servant, to bring Jacob back to Him, order that Israel might be gathered to Him (For I am honored in the sight of the Lord and my God is my strength).

Romans 9:11-12 — Yet, before the twins were born or had done anything good or bad — in order that God's purpose in election might stand: not by works but by him who calls — she was told, "The older will serve the younger."

Again, these verses show that God views the pre-born in the womb as persons. No other conclusion is possible. We must agree with theologian John Frame that, "There is nothing in Scripture that even remotely suggests that the unborn child is anything less than a human person from the moment of conception" (7:147).

D. Scriptures Which Indicate Human Life Belongs to God, Not to Us, Prohibit Abortion

The Bible teaches that people ultimately belong to God because all men are created by Him.

The Scriptures teach that men are "the offspring of God" (Acts 17:29) and that "in Him we live and move and exist" (Acts 17:28). Malachi could ask, "Have we not all one Father? Did not one God create us? (Malachi 2:10).

The Scriptures teach that God "Himself gives to all life and breath and all things" (Acts 17:25) because He "made the world and all things in it" (Acts 17:24). Understanding this, Isaiah could say "O Lord, Thou art our Father, we are the clay, and Thou our potter, and all of us are the work of Thy hand" (Isaiah. 64:8).

The Psalmist could say, "The earth is the Lord's, and everything in it, the world, and all who live in it" (Psalm 24:1).

David said, "Yours, O Lord, is the greatness and the power and the glory and the majesty and the splendor, for everything in heaven and earth is yours. Yours, O Lord, is the kingdom; you are exalted as head over all" (I Chronicles 29:11).

Further, the Scriptures teach, "Your hands made me and formed me . . ." (Psalm 119:73) and "The Lord . . . forms the spirit of man within him . . ." (Zechariah 12:1).

God Himself makes the statement, "Behold, all souls are Mine; the soul of the Father as well as the soul of the son is Mine" (Ezekiel 18:4).

Since all life was created by God and belongs to Him, no one has the right to kill another human being (Exodus 20:13).

E. Scriptures That Teach We Must Defend and Protect the Weak, the Defenseless, the Innocent, the Needy, and the Unwanted Prohibit Abortion

Consider the following Scriptures which indicate God's concern for the weak, the needy, the defenseless and those who cannot speak on their own behalf.

> Proverbs 31:8-9—Speak up for those who cannot speak for themselves, for the rights of all who are destitute. Speak up and judge fairly; defend the rights of the poor and needy.

> Psalm 82:2-4—How long will you defend the unjust and show partiality to the wicked? Defend the cause of the weak and fatherless; maintain the rights of the poor and oppressed. Rescue the weak and needy; deliver them from the hand of the wicked.

The Bible is full of Scriptures like this. There can be no doubt that they also apply to the innocent unborn who are the most defenseless, innocent and needy. Indeed, God will hold us accountable for their welfare:

> Rescue those being led away to death; hold back those staggering toward slaughter. If you say, "But we knew nothing

about this," does not he who weighs the heart perceive it? Does not he who guards your life know it? Will he not repay each person according to what he has done? (Proverbs 24:11-12)

In fact, numerous Scriptures condemn the killing of innocent life. Many of the following Scriptures also apply to those who perform abortions.

Proverbs 6:16-19—There are six things the Lord hates, seven that are detestable to him: haughty eyes, a lying tongue, hands that shed innocent blood, a heart that devises wicked schemes, feet that are quick to rush into evil, a false witness who pours out lies and a man who stirs up dissension among brothers.

Proverbs 17:5—He who mocks the poor shows contempt for their Maker; whoever gloats over disaster will not go unpunished.

Proverbs 12:6—The words of the wicked lie in wait for blood, but the speech of the upright rescues them.

Deuteronomy 27:25—"Cursed is he who accepts a bribe to strike down an innocent person." And all the people shall say, "Amen."

Deuteronomy 19:10—Do this so that innocent blood will not be shed in your land, which the Lord your God is giving you as your inheritance, and so that you will not be guilty of bloodshed.

Isaiah 1:15—When you spread out your hands in prayer, I will hide my eyes from you; even if you offer many prayers, I will not listen. Your hands are full of blood.

Isaiah 59:2-3, 4b, 7b—But your iniquities have separated you from your God; your sins have hidden his face from you, so that he will not hear. For your hands are stained with blood, your fingers with guilt. Your lips have spoken lies, and your tongue mutters wicked things. . . . They rely on empty arguments and speak lies; they conceive trouble and give birth to evil. . . . Their thoughts are evil thoughts; ruin and destruction mark their ways.

Jeremiah 22:17—But your eyes and your heart are intent only upon your own dishonest gain, and on shedding innocent blood and on practicing oppression and extortion.

Luke 17:2—It would be better for him if a millstone were hung around his neck and he were thrown into the sea, than that he should cause one of these little ones to stumble.

Hebrews 4:13—Nothing in all creation is hidden from God's sight. Everything is uncovered and laid bare before the eyes of him to whom we must give account.

F. Scriptures Which Indicate God Has a Plan Even for the Handicapped and Deformed Prohibit Abortion

Scriptures teach that God values those who are deformed or handicapped: "Who has made man's mouth? Or, who makes him dumb or deaf or seeing or blind? Is it not I, the Lord?" (Exodus 4:11). Isaiah warns: "Woe to him who quarrels with his Maker, to him who is but a potsherd [piece of clay] among the potsherds on the ground. Does the clay say to the potter, 'What are you making'? Does your work say, 'He has no hands'? Woe to him who says to his father, 'What have you begotten?' or to his mother, 'What have you brought to birth?' This is what the Lord says—the Holy One of Israel, and its Maker: Concerning things to come, do you question me about my children, or give me orders about the work of my hands?" (Isaiah 45:9-11).

The Lord Jesus Christ taught that the man born blind from birth was born that way in order to glorify God (John 9:1-4). If a person's deformity can bring glory to God, who are we to kill such persons and thereby prevent them from fulfilling God's plan for their lives?

Can one imagine Jesus accepting the idea of denying life to the handicapped or deformed? Did He not teach: "See that you do not despise one of these little ones, for I say to you, that their angels in heaven continually behold the face of My Father who is in heaven. . . . Thus it is not the will of your Father who is in heaven that one of these little ones perish" (Matthew 18:10, 14). All of these verses and more demonstrate that the Bible is not silent on denying life to the unwanted or unloved who are handicapped (cf. Job 33:4; 32:8; Isaiah 42:5; 44:24).

The act of abortion was considered an act of murder and completely unacceptable to both Jews and Christians (1:49-87). The opposition to abortion in the early Church was so pronounced there was simply no need for an explicit command. Princeton University professor Bruce Metzger refers to "the opposition of the early church to contemporary practices of abortion. It is really remarkable how uniform and how pronounced was the early Christian opposition to abortion" (1:84).

Indeed, the very reason the early Church was so opposed to abortion was the clearly discernible Biblical facts and principles we *have already* discussed.

G. Scriptures Which Indicate that the Personhood of Christ Was Present from Conception Prohibit Abortion

Another way to decide whether abortion is a justifiable practice is to think through the implications of the Incarnation of Jesus Christ. The question is, at what point was the personhood of Jesus present?

In brief, it *had* to be present at the point of conception. Both the New Testament and the doctrinal creeds of the Church affirm that God became man at the point of conception. The Eternal Son of God became Incarnate in Mary's womb. Christ's personal history on earth began not when He was "born of the virgin" but when He was "conceived by the Holy Spirit" (Luke 1:31, 35).

It is significant that God chose to begin the process of incarnation at the point of conception rather than at some other point. But Christ "had to be made like his brethren in all things" (Hebrews 2:17); His human history, like ours, had to begin at conception.

Lawyers Herbert T. Krimmel and Martin J. Foley argue that because Jesus was fully present at conception so must every other person be as well:

Now, given the facts established by Holy Scripture that (a) Christ was fully God and fully man and (b) Christ was conceived by the Holy Ghost, our argument can be stated succinctly:

1. "Conception" literally means the process which terminates the initial presence in the womb of that which is conceived (i.e., the single cell entity referred to in biological terms as a zygote). Consequently, when one says that Mary conceived by the activity of the Holy Ghost, one must mean that which the Holy Ghost produced in and through conception was the initial presence of the zygote.

2. The zygote the Holy Ghost brought about in Mary's womb was Jesus Christ, true God and true man, in His human nature like man in all things except for sin.

3. If Jesus (true God and true man) was present in His mother's womb from the first moment of His conception, then it follows that other men must also be alive and existing as human beings from the first moments of their conceptions; for unless they are the same as Jesus in this respect of their human nature, He would not be like them in every essential human respect except for sin. This is to say, then, that a human being must be fully present as such from the moment of conception. (34:12-13)

Finally, Hebrews 10:5 refers to the body that God prepared for Jesus which can only refer to His body in the womb. "Therefore, when Christ came into the world, He said: 'Sacrifice and offering you did not desire but a body you prepared for me.'" (see Isaiah 49:1-7).

H. Scriptures That Speak of God Giving Man a "Soul" Prohibit Abortion

Those reading their Bible through the centuries have learned that the human soul is a gift given by God. For some Christians, though, the issue of when the soul infuses the body has become a key point relating to the abortion controversy. Whenever the soul infuses the body, full human life is present. But a debate developed around the Scriptures that describe when God implants the soul into the body.

Some have argued that the Scriptures describe this point as being when the unborn fetus comes into existence at conception, others at viability, and still others have said it is at birth. Additional arguments then developed around the questions: Is the soul inherited from the parents and immediately present at conception, or given by God independent of the parents' sexual union sometime after the body is formed in the womb?

The reason these questions are important is because if the soul does not enter the body until sometime after conception, then some would argue that perhaps early abortions are permissible. If it can be shown that the soul is present from conception, then abortion is never permissible.

Christians who have argued that the soul is created individually by God and placed into the baby's body some point between conception and birth have been known as "Creationists." Those Christians who argue that each person derives his soul and his body at conception from his parents' sexual union are called "Traducians."

The following Bible verses are cited as proof by the
"Creationists" that God created man's spirit, or his soul, individually and placed it into the body at some point between conception and birth:

> Genesis 2:7—And the Lord God formed man of the dust of
> the ground, and breathed into his nostrils the breath of life;
> and man became a living soul.(KJV)

> Ecclesiastes 12:7—Then shall the dust [of which God made
> man's body] return to the earth as it was, and the spirit shall
> return to God who gave it.(KJV)

> Zechariah 12:1—Thus declares the Lord who stretches out the
> heavens, lays the foundation of the earth, and forms the spirit
> of man within him.

> (Also see Isaiah 42:5, Isaiah 57:16 and Hebrews 12:9.)

But after reading these verses cited by the Creationists, we
must admit that we do not know from these texts that the fetus
has been endowed with a soul by God from the time of conception, viability, or at birth. All we know is that God is the One
who gives man a soul. So these verses by themselves do not
help solve the question of, "Is abortion permissible?"

Now let us turn to the other viewpoint that is held by those
Christians called "Traducians" who maintain that the soul derives by natural laws of propagation from one's parents. In other
words, they believe each person inherits his soul from his parents just as much as he does his body. They point to the following Biblical texts:

> Genesis 1:27, 28—So God created man in his own image, in
> the image of God created he him; male and female created he
> them. And God blessed them, and God said unto them, Be
> fruitful, and multiply.(KJV)

> Genesis 5:1-3—When God created man, He made him in the
> likeness of God. He created them male and female and blessed

them . . . When Adam had lived 130 years, he had a son in his own likeness, in his own image; and he named him Seth.

Hebrews 7:9, 10—And, so to speak, through Abraham even Levi, who received tithes, paid tithes, for he was still *in the loins of his father* when Melchizedek met him. (Emphasis added)

But after reading these verses cited by Christians arguing the Traducian viewpoint we must ask, "Is it not possible that both positions present a bit of the truth and that the body originates from the parents while the soul originates from God?" Traducians are forced to admit that there are many verses that support the Creationist viewpoint—that God alone gives the soul. Creationists must also admit that there are some Bible verses that imply that though God gives the soul, He may have used the means of human propagation to place it in the body.

The key point in terms of the abortion debate is that anyone honestly looking at these verses must conclude that Scripture has not clearly presented the exact moment when the soul is given, only that God does give the soul to man.

Theologians such as Paul K. Jewett, Kenneth Kantzer and John Warwick Montgomery agree. They have concluded that it is not possible to access from the Bible one precise view of when the soul was united with the body. But as we shall see, when these Scripture verses are added to Exodus 21:22-25, the Bible makes it absolutely clear that the life of the unborn child in the womb is as valuable in God's sight as an adult outside the womb. This causes us to believe that from the point of conception, the soul is present even though no direct Scripture can be cited. We noted earlier that from conception onward the value of life is equal at every point and further, equal in value to adult life. Our conclusion, then, must be that the soul exists from the point of conception, otherwise it would not have equal value in God's eyes.

I. Scriptures That Prove That God Values the Fetus as Much as an Adult: Exodus 21:22-25 Prohibit Abortion

If, as we have seen, the Bible gives no precise answer on the origin of the soul, or the exact time at which the soul is placed in the human body by God, we can be sure that the Bible makes it absolutely clear that the life of the unborn child in the womb is held by God to be a person and valued as highly as an adult.

There are Christians who assert that even though many of the Bible verses we have studied talk about the value of unborn life in the womb, there is a higher value placed on children at birth than those who are developing in the womb. But Holy Scripture does not give us a precise value to be set on the human fetus at each stage of the fertilized egg up through viability, to birth, and a neatly categorized numerical value on each alternative evil with which we may be faced if one aborts the fetus at that stage. Rather, the Bible teaches that the fetus in the womb at any stage is valued as highly as any adult life.

Where does the Bible teach this? Exodus 21:22-25 states,

> If men who are fighting hit a pregnant woman and she gives birth prematurely but there is no serious injury, the offender must be fined whatever the woman's husband demands and the court allows. But if there is serious injury, you are to take life for life, eye for eye, tooth for tooth, hand for hand, foot for foot, burn for burn, wound for wound, bruise for bruise.

Distinguished Jewish exegete Umberto Cassuto interprets and translates Exodus 21:22-25 in his celebrated *Commentary of the Book of Exodus:*

> When men strive together and they hurt unintentionally a woman with child, and her children come forth but no mischief happens—that is, the woman and the children do not die—the one who hurt her shall surely be punished by a fine.

> But if any mischief happened, that is, if the woman dies or
> the children die, then you shall give life for life. (120:275)

Keil and Delitzsch in their Old Testament commentary on
the book of Exodus explain that the passage demands exactly
the same penalty for injuring the mother as the child (123:134-
135).

In the 60s and early 70s some Evangelical theologians interpreted Exodus 21:22 wrongly. One well-known Evangelical
translated this passage as follows:

> When men struggle together and one of them pushes a preg-
> nant woman and she suffers a miscarriage but no other harm
> happens, he shall be fined according as the woman's husband
> may exact from him. . . . But if harm does ensue, then you
> shall impose soul for soul. . . . Clearly, then, in contrast to the
> mother, the fetus is not reckoned as a soul [*nephesh*]. (121:11)

Under this interpretation, if the fetus was valued as a full
human being, then the law would have required capital punishment. But, since none was fixed in this verse, apparently the
fetus was not valued as a full human. Evangelical theologians
espousing this view did not imply that the fetus was of no value,
but the value would not be equal to that of the mother's life.

But these Evangelicals erred in their interpretation and later
changed their minds. The Hebrew is clear that if either the
mother or fetus suffers minor harm, then a minor harm should
be assessed; but, if further injury results to either mother or
fetus, such as death, then the fine or punishment is equal to a
life for a life, and an eye for an eye. There is absolutely no
ground to differentiate between the mother or the child in this
context if we keep to the rights of language.

Distinguished Hebrew scholar Dr. Gleason Archer has
stated about this passage:

> There is no ambiguity here whatever. What is required is that
> if there should be an injury either to the mother or to her
> children, the injury shall be avenged by a like injury to the

assailant. If it involves the life, the *nephesh*, of the premature baby, then the assailant shall pay for it with his life. There is no second class status attached to the fetus under this rule. The fetus is just as valuable as the mother. It is as if he were a normally delivered child or an older person. The penalty is life for life. (122:3)

In his article "Lex Talionis and the Human Fetus," Meredith G. Kline, Professor of Old Testament at Westminster Theological Seminary in California also argues forcefully that this Scripture underscores the personhood of the fetus as well as its equal value with adult human life. His detailed arguments and exegesis should permanently lay to rest the idea that this passage justifies assigning a lesser value to pre-born life than to adult life. A quick summary of his conclusions may be noted:

This law found in Exodus 21:22-25 turns out to be perhaps the most decisive positive evidence in Scripture that the fetus is to be regarded as a living person. . . . No matter whether one interprets the first or second penalty to have reference to a miscarriage, there is no difference in the treatments according to the fetus and the woman. Either way the fetus is regarded as a living person, so that to be criminally responsible for the destruction of the fetus is to forfeit one's life. . . . The fetus, at any stage of development, is, in the eyes of this law, a living being, for life (*nephesh*) is attributed to it. . . . Consistently in the relevant data of Scripture a continuum of identity is evident between the fetus and the person subsequently born and Exodus 21:22-25 makes it clear that this prenatal human being is to be regarded as a separate and distinct human life. (36:75, 83, 88-89)

The sixth commandment, "Thou shalt not kill" (Hebrew: murder) refers to every act of murder: child, wife, husband, stranger, self, etc. Since it is scientifically established that the fetus *is* a human being, the commandment applies to abortion as well. "Thou shalt not kill" is equivalent to "Thou shalt not commit abortion."

Of course, we should remember that in any culture the death penalty is the prerogative of the state alone; never of the individual. The only responsibility of the individual is confession of his/her sin and restoration to God.

In addition, a variety of Biblical teachings collectively prohibit abortion. For example, the fact that every person has value and dignity because he/she is created in God's image should influence our view of abortion. Also, repeated Biblical teaching on God's special care for the poor, the innocent and the defenseless bears on the abortion question.

Further, the Bible clearly teaches that men and women in the act of procreation are co-workers with God in the process of bringing new life into existence. Then, too, the Scriptures teach that God forms the child in the womb, that the child is an "artwork" of God Himself. Finally, we find in the Bible that all human life is absolutely unique, precious, and loved by God. Those who destroy human life are held accountable by God.

All of the above and a great deal more indicate that the Bible is not silent on abortion. To the contrary, a Biblical understanding of God, man, procreation and conception, gestation, and life itself reveals that far from being silent on abortion, the Bible teaches that abortion is a crime against both God and man.

Questions for Discussion

1. Discuss several Scriptures which reveal that God views the fetus as a person.

2. Discuss Scriptures which prove that God does not make distinctions between pre-born life and children. Why do you think God made no distinctions here?

3. How does the continuity of life from conception to old age affect the abortion issue? Defend your answer scientifically and scripturally.

4. Cite and discuss several Scriptures proving that God Himself personally relates to the unborn. Pay special attention to Psalm 139; examine several different translations. What does it mean that God calls men into service "from the womb" and how does this relate to abortion?

5. Discuss Scriptures which prove that human life belongs to God first. Does abortion usurp the prerogative of God?

6. Many Scriptures tell Christians to defend the cause of the needy, innocent and unwanted. How do we know these Scriptures also apply to the unborn?

7. Are those born with physical or mental deformities valuable to God? What are the implications of assigning value or meaning on the basis of degrees of perfection?

8. How does the Incarnation of Jesus Christ relate to abortion and the issue of when human life begins?

9. Can either the "Creation" or "Traducian" view be proven from Scripture? If not, why does this not disprove the idea that human life begins at conception and that the soul exists from conception?

10. Discuss Exodus 21:22-25. Show why these verses prove that human life in the womb is equal in value to adult life.

DO THE SCRIPTURES REVEAL THAT BOTH GOD AND MAN ARE "CO-WORKERS" IN THE PRODUCTION OF A HUMAN BEING?

P erhaps the strongest scriptural and theological argument against abortion is this: Biblically, God Himself is said to create the child in the womb. If true, then those who have an abortion are not merely destroying "tissue" or "protoplasm" or even "merely" a human person, but an actual work of God Himself. If true, can anyone feel this is insignificant?

Four lines of argument serve to prove the fact that it is God in conjunction with a man and a woman who is the Creator of life in the womb.

Fact 1: Some Forty Times in Scripture the Bible Refers to Conception as the "Start" of Life

For example:

In the Genesis narratives alone, the phrase "conceived and bore" is found eleven times. The close pairing of the two words clearly emphasizes conception, not birth, as the starting point of life. Biblical passages revealing the divine role in conception simply serve to confirm that it is more than just a biological phenomenon. The start of a human life is clearly a special occurrence in which God takes part. . . . (7:136)

Fact 2: The Scripture Teaches That God Both Opens and Closes the Womb

Consider the following Scriptures where God Himself is seen as active in the event of conception itself:

Ruth 4:13 — The Lord *enabled her to conceive,* and she gave birth to a son. (Emphasis added)

1 Samuel 1:5, 10, 20 — But to Hannah he would give a double portion, for he loved Hannah, but the Lord *had closed her womb.* . . . And she, greatly distressed, prayed to the Lord and wept bitterly. . . . And it came about in due time, after Hannah had conceived, that she gave birth to a son; and she named him Samuel, saying, "Because I have asked him of the Lord." (Emphasis added)

Exodus 23:25-26 — But you shall serve the Lord your God, and He will bless your bread and your water; and I will remove sickness from among your midst. There shall be *no one miscarrying or barren* in your land. *I will fulfill the number of your days.* (cf. Deuteronomy 7:13-15) (Emphasis added)

Genesis 29:31-32 — Now the Lord saw that Leah was unloved, and *He opened her womb,* but Rachel was barren. And Leah conceived and bore a son and named him Reuben, for she said, "Because the Lord has seen my affliction. . . ." (Emphasis added)

Genesis 30:2, 22-23 — Then Jacob's anger burned against Rachel, and he said, "Am I in the place of God, who has *withheld from you* the fruit of the womb?" . . . Then God remembered Rachel, and God gave heed to her and *opened her womb*. So she conceived and bore a son. . . . (Emphasis added)

Fact 3: The Bible Describes Children as an Added, Precious Gift to Marriage

Psalm 127:3-5a—Sons are a heritage from the Lord, children a reward from him. Like arrows in the hands of a warrior are sons born in one's youth. Blessed is the man whose quiver is full of them.

Psalm 128:3-4—Your wife will be like a fruitful vine within your house; your sons will be like olive shoots around your table. Thus is the man blessed who fears the Lord.

Fact 4: God Himself Actively Creates and Molds Life in the Womb

Dietrich Bonhoffer, the Lutheran theologian who was executed by the Nazis for his opposition to Hitler, said the following of abortion: "The simple fact is that God intended to create a human being and . . . this human being has been deliberately deprived of his life. And that is nothing but murder" (6:128).

Given modern man's naturalistic and evolutionary approach to life, we suppose that the power of reproduction lies solely within the ovum and sperm and is entirely controlled by the genetic code. But the process by which a single cell is multiplied into a thousand million cells which then organize themselves into incredibly complex physical structures (an eye, brain, circulatory system, etc.) is a process that continues to completely mystify even the most brilliant researchers. Biblically, it is clear that God Himself is involved in the process. Consider the following Scriptures:

Job 10:8a—Thy hands fashioned and made me altogether.

Job 10:10-12—Didst thou not pour me out like milk, and cur-
dle me like cheese; clothe me with skin and flesh, and knit
me together with bones and sinews? Thou hast granted me
life and loving kindness; and thy care has preserved my spirit.

Job 31:15—Did not He who made me in the womb [also]
make him, and the same one fashion us in the womb?

Psalm 119:73a—Thy hands made me and fashioned me.

Psalm 139:13-16—For Thou didst form my inward parts;
Thou didst weave me in my mother's womb. I will give
thanks to Thee, for I am fearfully and wonderfully made;
wonderful are Thy works, and my soul knows it very well.
My frame was not hidden from Thee, when I was made in
secret, And skillfully wrought in the depths of the earth.
Thine eyes have seen my unformed substance; And in Thy
book they were all written, The days that were ordained for
me when as yet there was not one of them.

Jeremiah 1:5a—Before I formed you in the womb I knew you.

Ephesians 2:10a—For we are His workmanship . . .

The above Scriptures indicate that the creation of man is not
something that simply happens at a point of time but that it is a
continuous divine activity from conception onward. Thus:

The Bible makes it clear that human creation was not something that just took place in the past; rather, it continues. Eve
is quoted as saying, "I have created [*qanah*] a man with the
Lord" (Genesis 4:1, author's translation). She was certainly
not implying that Adam had nothing to do with Cain's birth;
Genesis 4:1a makes that clear: "Now Adam knew Eve his
wife, and she conceived. . . ." These examples sufficiently
demonstrate that birth is considered a creative process involving man, woman, and God.

God's ongoing work in the creation of new life is further illustrated in statements where God reminds Israel that He
"formed" them (Isaiah 43:1, 7; 44:21) and declares, "I formed
[you] for myself." (Isaiah 43:21)

In these passages from Isaiah, the word rendered "formed" is *yasar,* as it is in the oft quoted Jeremiah 1:5: "Before I formed you in the womb, I knew you." The choice of *yasar* in these texts is deliberate, for it connects the creating of individuals to God's "forming" activity witnessed in Genesis 2:7.

Instead of using clay, God uses human instruments to continue the process of creation that he set in motion by his creative activity and then by his command to "be fruitful and multiply" (Gen. 1:28). On this note, Babbage (1963, 15) aptly says, "God permits man to share in the joyous task of creation." (1:55, 56)

And:

Does not abortion deny the holy nature of conception, the divine opening of the womb? Does not the attempt to undervalue the importance of conception for the beginning of human life go contrary to the clear teaching of Scripture? And does not the contemporary attitude toward the unborn as an inconvenience or burden fly directly in the face of their being a blessing from God? (7:139-40)

When a child is aborted, are we not destroying a literal creation of God?

How then does God feel about abortion? In the late 1960s, John Weldon, one of the authors of this book, remembers when radical students bombed a professor's office, completely destroying seven years of his irreplaceable research. The professor was shattered.

What right did the radicals have to destroy this man's work? None: but then, how about abortionists? Would "pro-choice" individuals allow others to destroy another person's artwork simply because they didn't want it around? The answer is no. But why will they demand the right to destroy God's "artwork," precious human beings, which are far more valuable than mere research or paint on a canvas?

Ultimately, the creation of new life in the Old Testament is attributed to God the Creator, who is both Designer and Artist. What would a human artist think if he was working on a masterpiece and someone destroyed his work? Even though not complete, the expected reaction would no doubt be anger and rage. If this is the reaction of the earthly artist, how much more intense would be God's revulsion at the destruction of a fetus, his masterpiece that is being formed!

. . . The reality of an artist's hurt and anguish over the willful destruction of his handiwork became apparent to me during an exhibition of an art student at Wheaton College in the early 1970s. Someone took a can of spray paint to a couple of canvases that met with that person's disapproval. The artist was understandably crushed. This deliberate destruction of an art object expressed a lack of respect for both the artist and the art. So, too, the indiscriminate destruction of human fetuses declares precisely the same attitude toward God and man. (1:56-57)

In conclusion, the continued purposeful destruction of God's handiwork can only provoke His wrath.

Questions for Discussion

1. Give several Scriptures proving that God and man are "co-creators" in the production of human life. Why is this important to the abortion controversy? Is abortion destroying a work of God?

2. Why does this matter?

HOW DO THE THEOLOGICAL IMPLICATIONS OF MAN'S "CREATION IN THE IMAGE OF GOD" RELATE TO ABORTION?

T he Bible teaches in Genesis 1:27: "And God created man in His own image, in the image of God He created him; male and female He created them." Further, in verse 31 God calls His creation, including man, "very good." Biblically then, man is not the chance product of impersonal matter as the materialists and evolutionists claim (124). Rather, man is created in God's image, providing him with dignity and value as man — which no one else has the right to destroy.

In his *History of European Morals,* historian William E. H. Lecky (1955, pages 20-24) observes that one of the fortunate consequences of the rise of Christianity was the understanding among people that man was made in the image of God. He notes that with this understanding, abortion was on the way out (6:123).

It is not difficult to see why. A poll of those who are of the pro-choice camp would undoubtedly reveal the great majority are materialists who deny man's creation by God. In fact, several lines of evidence can be produced showing the logical influence of materialistic, evolutionary thinking upon the modern abortion holocaust (e.g., 1:90-91; 7:39-40, 46-49, cf. 124).

For example, it is seriously argued today by some evolutionary scientists that the child undergoes the various stages of human evolution during its development in the womb. This scientifically discredited concept is termed *ontogeny recapitulates phylogeny.* Because the fetus is allegedly a "lower form" of life in its early stages and not human, it is therefore not murder to kill it since it is merely a "fish" or a "reptile."

For example, the *Los Angeles Times* (January 29, 1989, part V) cites one scientist who believes,

> From a single primordial cell, the conceptus progresses through being something of a protozoan, a fish, a reptile, a bird, a primate and ultimately a human being. There is a difference of opinion among scientists about the time during a pregnancy when a human being can be said to emerge. But there is general agreement that this does not happen until after the end of the first trimester.

The modern rise in acceptance of abortion is much more easily understood if contemporary man believes there is no God and that man ultimately has no meaning or value. After all, people who truly believed God existed and that man was a wholly unique and very special creation of God, would find it—one would think—extremely difficult to deliberately support the destruction of such life. In fact, we suspect the abortion debate today is largely a debate between two fundamentally hostile camps: theists and atheists (or materialists).

Table 40.1 shows the two different world views in relation to life in the womb:

Table 40:1	
PRE-BORN CHILDREN	
Abortion View ("Pro-Choice")	**Biblical or Christian View ("Pro-Life")**
The fetus is protoplasm or tissue; a nonhuman or nonperson.	The fetus is a human being, a living person.
Naturalistic evolutionary view of conception and gestation; conception and pregnancy are profane.	Men and women are co-creators with God in the process of conception; conception and pregnancy are sacred and holy. God molds and fashions the child in the womb.
Human life or personhood begins at viability, birth or some other arbitrary point.	Human life and personhood begins at conception.
Conception is a process.	Conception is the point the sperm and egg unite.
Children are a burden or an inconvenience.	Children are a gift from the Lord.
Conceived life is viewed as temporal only, based on materialistic presuppositions; no soul at conception.	Conceived life is not merely temporal, but also eternal; the soul exists at conception.
No image of God in the fetus.	The fetus contains the image of God.

Philosopher David K. Clark discusses how the denial of man's divine image logically repudiates the sanctity of life and opens the door for abortion, infanticide and euthanasia (37:93-112; cf. ref. 103).

For example, writing in the journal *Pediatrics* for July, 1983 (p. 129) Peter Singer alleges:

We can no longer base our ethics on the idea that human beings are a special form of creation, made in the image of God. . . . Our better understanding of our nature has bridged the gulf that was once thought to lie between ourselves and other species, so why should we believe that the mere fact

that a being is a member of the species *homo sapiens* endows
its life with some unique, almost infinite value? (37:97-98)

In our last section we saw that Biblically, God and men
were co-workers in the production of life; that life was much
more than solely the natural product of procreation. Indeed,
when one considers how minuscule is our understanding of the
process of conception and gestation, ruling out divine co-
creatorship *a priori* would appear to be unwise in the least. For
example, modern research

has created the impression that with some understanding of
DNA the mystery of [cell] differentiation—even of life itself—has been solved. The fact is, however, that the path
from the genes to the configuration of the organism is still *not
even discernible* by way of suggestion. What is going on between so-called genetic information in the life process of configuration *is still completely unknown.* Therefore, it is still
questionable to present the genetic substance as the text of a
book, as it were, already containing all directions for the differentiation at each moment of the development and for every
part of the organism. If we imagine, for instance, the genetic
substance as a kind of cookbook, it would have value only if
a cook were to use it, but it remains entirely unexplained who
in the system of cells this cook is. (11:13-15, emphasis added)

The "Cook," of course, is God, who is actively present in
the production of a unique new life.

Because man is made in the image of God, life is by definition sacred and should not be destroyed. The capital punishment
prescribed in Genesis 9:6 is based exclusively upon the image of
God in man, that is, on the basis of man's divine value and
importance: "Whoever sheds man's blood, By man his blood
shall be shed, For in the image of God He made man" (Genesis
9:6). In Numbers 35:33 God warns: "You shall not pollute the
land in which you are; for blood [murder] pollutes the land and
no expiation can be made for the land for the blood that is shed
on it, except by the blood of him who shed it."

The "image of God" is not only something present at conception due to the natural/supernatural nature of the process involved, but the image of God is also something that a person grows into as well. The "image of God" probably involves a great deal more than any theologian has yet considered; however, one thing is certain: it is only fully complete when the redeemed are finally "like Him" in eternity (1 John 3:2).

But it may also be true that God's image is most fully revealed when, through the marriage union, there is the creation of new life. In all eternity, few human acts will match that one, single, profound reality—the bringing into existence of an eternal human being. Thus, the "image of God" is ultimately a part of the creative power supplied to the fetus, providing spiritual power for it to develop in the manner that it does—not only through birth but also through adulthood, death and eventual glorification (1:90). It is even suggested that the genetic combination of ovum and sperm produces a human being not because of the genetic process per se but from the fact of "the image of God incarnate in the genetics of conception" (1:91). Thus:

> From a philosophical point of view, the distinction I am making is analogous to the Aristotelian distinction between form and substance: the human parents provide the substance and the divine image provides the form of humanness. Both form and substance are present at conception, but both grow into the manifestation of the image of God. (1:91)

And it is here that we see the full horror of abortion. In James 3:9 we are warned not even to curse other men because all men are made in the image of God. But what abortion does is not only to destroy the image of God, but in addition, it prevents the image of God from ever being fully manifest in this life (1:91):

> We conclude, then, that abortion is a very serious sin against the purposes of God in creation and should be permitted only

in those extremely rare cases where the life of the mother is
at real risk! Then abortion is the lesser of two evils. (1:91)

Questions for Discussion

1. How does the "image of God" in man relate to abortion? How have naturalistic, evolutionary assumptions
   helped conceal this fact?

2. Give seven differences in attitude toward the unborn
   among most theists and atheists? What difference does
   it make?

3. How might abortion contribute to euthanasia and infanticide?

ABORTION: WHAT CAN INDIVIDUAL CHRISTIANS AND THEIR CHURCHES DO?

TEN STRATEGIES
FOR ACTION

There are many things individual Christians and churches can and should do on behalf of innocent individuals still in the womb.

What we should remember is that even a single individual can have a far greater impact than he or she believes possible. Church history is full of average men and women whose single vision and dedication to a cause produced dramatic results. Even where God does not lead a person to full-time effort, devoting merely one hour per week can, when multiplied, become a powerful agent for change.

The abortion lobby is doing all in its power to preserve its interests. If concerned individuals do nothing, the abortion lobby will win the day and the late 1990's will see our nation approaching or exceeding 50 million abortions. Below we present a brief list of ten possible strategies which we would like you to consider doing.

1. Pray

Every Christian can pray that God would work to change the current situation. Scripture promises that prayer "is powerful and effective" (James 5:16). There is no reason Christians cannot be more active in prayer—organizationally and individually.

Further, Christians can pray specifically for guidance as to how God might personally lead them to be involved in their church and community.

2. Begin Letter-Writing Campaigns

Most Christians do not realize that if people in the church took only a few minutes a day to write their elected representatives, this alone would have dramatic results. But much more can be done. Letters can be written to editors of local newspapers and national magazines and to local radio stations whenever abortion myths are promoted. Local television stations should always be called or written to and sometimes approached requesting equal time for pro-life concerns. National network officials should always be contacted if complaints are justified concerning biased, erroneous or unfair reporting.

3. Vote

Christians can support candidates who are committed to protecting unborn human lives and oppose pro-choice candidates. Also, Christians should let them know why they will not vote for them and why they think the abortion issue deserves their reevaluation. If the 40 million or so Christians would actively get involved on behalf of children in the womb, there is no doubt abortion would legally be stopped.

4. Organize Local Rallies

Christians can join in peaceful demonstrations or mobilize small demonstrations on behalf of the unborn in their town. They should always inform the media of the event and prepare intelligent answers for their views. Rallies or demonstrations whether of 50, 500, or larger have an impact at the local level, generate interest, and can become a catalyst for unexpected benefits. It is not necessary to have large numbers of people. Most of the time, just a handful of pro-choice people turn out and end up giving their views on the news. You can do the same.

5. Organize Support Groups for Pregnant Women

At the local level, Christians and churches must begin to start and support a wide variety of pregnancy crisis and counseling ministries. Society today has largely abandoned its women.

The Church must take up the slack here or suffer the consequences. Women must be helped through the birth process and beyond with financial, emotional and spiritual encouragement and counseling. The church must recognize and act upon the fact that merely overturning *Roe v. Wade* or establishing a Constitutional "Right to Life" Amendment will not solve the entire problem. Recriminalization of abortion must not become a new form of abandonment of women.

Positive alternatives to abortion must be given top priority in American social policy. This should be achieved in such a manner that the irresponsible sexual behavior leading to pregnancy must be discouraged.

The Christians and their church can be involved in as many (9:322-324) different ways as possible:

- Financial aid should be available to help pregnant women through their pregnancy, including meeting the medical expenses.

- Contacts should be made with obstetricians, gynecologists and counselors, informing them that the church stands ready to aid the woman through her pregnancy.

- Emotional, spiritual, legal and medical counseling should be available without cost.

- Counseling centers, shelters and adoption agencies should be established or expanded throughout the nation.

- Work should be done to have institutional barriers against unwed mothers dropped. For example, birth certificates should not stigmatize both child and mother as "illegitimate." The more social support a woman receives and the more normal her life, the greater the chance for a healthy adjustment to her pregnancy and a positive outcome.

- Support programs must continue after the child is born.

- Every available means must be undertaken in the church to change irresponsible sexual behavior. Adult men and women, *especially* men, must take more responsibility for their actions. Parents should not commit the sin of ostracizing or abandoning their teenagers who are pregnant. Abandoned teenagers find it far easier to abandon their pregnancy than if they are given the love, understanding, encouragement and support of their families.

If programs such as the above are implemented in conjunction with a legal ban upon abortion, we can look forward to the day when illegal abortions can be reduced far below the pre-1973 level. The fact remains that the majority of women don't want an abortion. Most of them have been socially intimidated into feeling that they simply have no other choice.

6. Become Better Informed

Every person concerned about abortion can become better informed on the issues. Each person needs to become intellectually convinced and able to wield arguments in favor of that position.

The starred texts in the reference section are particularly important. We especially recommend Thomas W. Hilgers and Dennis J. Horan's (eds.) *Abortion and Social Justice* (101); Landrum B. Shettles' *Rites of Life: The Scientific Evidence for*

Life Before Birth (100); David C. Reardon's *Aborted Women: Silent No More* (9) and John T. Noonan Jr.'s *A Private Choice* (13). If only a few texts can be read on the subject, these should be considered. We also especially recommend Teri and Paul Reisser's, *Help for the Post Abortion Woman* (Zondervan 1989) which compassionately assists women to deal with the aftermath of an abortion.

In the last 200 years the Supreme Court has overturned itself over 100 times on decisions of moderate to major importance (25:32)! People who are concerned about abortion should not be intimidated by a decision of seven people or let it prevent them from expressing their convictions. That decision alone has already resulted in the slaughter of 26 million other people. Many texts in your home town library will document the fact that the justices' decision was legally, morally and medically incorrect (13:1-192; 101:301-320; 7:19-20, 33).

In addition, such information should have a practical result. We must not only work for the overthrow of *Roe v. Wade.* To insure that the Supreme Court will not once again change its mind and reverse its reversal, the church must also work for a Constitutional Amendment guaranteeing the right to life of the unborn. Constitutional Amendments are very difficult to enact. However, the gravity of the issue more than justifies the attempt.

7. Mobilize Individual Christians and, If Possible, Your Church for Action

There are numerous ways that churches can become active at the local and national level to oppose abortion — in fact, one text lists 99 different approaches (40).

Certainly every church can have a "right to life" or "pro-life" committee which will coordinate activity at the local level as well as pursue state and national goals. Letters need to be written to local, state and federal representatives. Letters should be written to the editorial columns of newspapers and magazines. Individual companies supporting the abortion industry can be boycotted.

What must be countered is the current reversal of priorities within the church. For example, Christians will support "health and wealth" churches by the millions but ignore the innocent, needy, and poor in the womb. Between 1968 and 1989, Christians have signed petitions by the millions to "stop" an alleged campaign to take religious broadcasts off the air. Although a brief attempt was made at regulation, it was withdrawn. But although Christians have written millions of letters to stop a nonexistent threat, they have not written enough to stop a real campaign that has destroyed 26 million children forever. How can Christians spend millions of man hours in behalf of a nonexistent cause and ignore a far greater issue? How can we allow liberal Protestant and Catholic theologians by the thousands to actively promote abortion when even atheists like Bernard Nathanson can see it is the willful destruction of human life? When Christians take the time to be informed on this subject and mobilize their churches, then the church will begin to exert its power. Is this something that you, the reader, need to pray about doing?

8. Support Pro-Life Organizations with Time and Finances

Many fine pro-life organizations exist which are already mobilized to educate and support. A few minutes on the phone can change a life. These organizations include the National Right to Life Committee (202-626-8800, lobbying efforts); Operation Rescue (404-421-9552, peaceful resistance); Bethany Christian Services (616-459-6273; 1-800-BETHANY, pregnancy counseling; adoption); Alternatives to Abortion International (407-277-1942; 914-683-0901, comprehensive service to pregnant women); Birthright International (1-800-848-5683; 609-848-1819; housing, medical, financial and other assistance to pregnant women); National Committee for Adoption (202-328-1200); The American Adoption Agency (202-638-1543); Women Exploited by Abortion (W.E.B.A.), (the W.E.B.A. has merged with Open A.R.M.S., Abortion Related Ministries, 206-839-8919); Christian Action Council (703-237-2100); American Life League (703-659-4171; 202-546-5550, lobbying); Americans Against Abortion (214-963-8676); National Pro-Family Coalition (202-546-5342); Right to Life Education Committee Media Impact Campaign (616-451-0225), etc.

Other crisis pregnancy programs are: Open Arms Ministries (206-435-3395); CAC Crisis Pregnancy Centers (703-237-2100); Pearson Foundation (314-652-5300; 800-633-2252); Prolife Action League (312-777-2525); PACE, Post Abortion Counseling and Education (703-237-2100).

These organizations have a great deal of useful material that can be made available to individuals and churches.

9. Organize Counter Demonstrations at Every Level to Oppose the Demonstrations of the Pro-Abortion Lobby

The pro-abortion lobby recognizes that winning small battles over abortion is the key to its long-term goals. Those representing pro-choice are gearing themselves for a major offensive against pro-life forces. Local newspapers, magazines, and the media in general need to be informed that every time and every place the abortion industry carries out demonstrations there will be counter demonstrations by those concerned for the unborn.

10. Should We Consider Placing Ourselves in Front of the Abortion Mills?

The issue raised by Operation Rescue is important. When a government permits social evil, are Christians morally bound to disobey the law to oppose it, or not? Below we present some of the arguments for and against this position.

Argument for:

Unfortunately, America may be so far down the path to destruction that perhaps only this kind of action will alter the current situation. As a young pregnant woman observed, "In this society we save whales, we save timber wolves, bald eagles and Coke bottles. Yet, everyone wanted me to throw away my baby" (5:35). Malcolm Muggeridge once noted, "Either life is always and in all circumstances sacred, or intrinsically of no account; it is inconceivable that it should be in some cases the one, and in some the other" (5:34).

But as former U.S. Surgeon General C. Everett Koop lamented, "It is quite possible that when the inevitable swing of the pendulum takes place and life once again becomes precious, it might be too late to stop the slide that will ultimately herald the decline and demise of our civilization" (5:43).

But because we cannot determine the future, we have no excuse for not acting now.

The battle cannot be won by pen and argument. It will not be won without great effort, sacrifice, and perhaps, blood. Historically, many peoples and nations have been liberated from cruel slavery and even genocide—but not without great cost. Even the delivery of the Israelite people from Egyptian bondage occurred only through the judgment of God.

President Lincoln reflected both upon the judgment of God and the terrible price the nation had paid to free the slave:

If we shall suppose that American slavery is one of those offenses which, in the providence of God, must needs come, but which, having continued through his appointed time, he now wills to remove, and that he gives to both North and South this terrible war, as the woe due to those by whom the offense came, shall we discern therein any departure from those divine attributes which the believers in a living God always ascribe to him?

Fondly do we hope — fervently do we pray — that this mighty scourge of war may speedily pass away. Yet, if God wills that it continue until all the wealth piled by the bondsmen's 250 years of unrequited toil shall be sunk, and until every drop of blood drawn with the lash shall be paid by another drawn with the sword, as was said 3,000 years ago, so still it must be said, "The judgments of the Lord are true and righteous altogether." (3:124, citing Paul Angle, *The Lincoln Reader,* New Brunswick, NJ, Rutgers University Press, 1947, pp. 492-493)

It has been pointed out that we are only deceiving ourselves if we believe the rights and freedom of the unborn will someday happen by quiet agreement of those in power. The rights of the unborn will need to be "purchased," but the purchase price has not yet been paid — far from it. "Solidarity with anyone headed for the slaughter naturally figures to be a costly business" (3:125). Thus:

Life for the unborn will never be durably defined in Washington until it is first defined at the door of the abortion clinic.

Law follows fact more than fact follows law. If I cannot defend a child's life at the moment of a child's death, I cannot convincingly defend the child's life in the courts, in the legislature, or in the pulpit. My failure to show solidarity with the child in real life puts the lie to my oral arguments.

Whether we like it or not, life is being defined every day of the week at the doors of America's abortion clinics, and the definition is a photocopy of *Roe v. Wade.* (3:125)

Should those concerned over the rights of the unborn really lay down their bodies in front of abortion clinics? Consider the following illustration (in 3:159-160).

Some of us may have even experienced a similar situation. A member of our family is ill. Suddenly, without warning, the illness worsens to the point where the individual's life is at risk. Paramedics are not available, so we place the person in our car and rush to the hospital, straight through red lights, breaking every speed limit posted. We know that the situation is severe enough that even seconds may mean the difference between life and death. Traveling eighty to one hundred miles an hour in a forty-mile-an-hour zone, we hear sirens and are pulled over by the police. We roll down the window and explain the situation to the officer, who immediately jumps on his motorcycle and escorts us at high speed to the hospital. As a result of our decisive action and that of the officer, we save the life of a loved one.

But wait a minute. What if that officer who stopped us had taken a look at our injured and dying loved one and merely grimly shaken his head, apologizing for the fact that he really didn't write the laws himself but only enforces them, and that it was his responsibility to arrest and prosecute those who violate speeding laws? What if the officer arrested us, took us to the station, fingerprinted us, and placed us in jail until our bail could be raised? What if he let our wife, husband or child perish in the back seat of the car?

Do we believe that enforcing the speeding laws at that point would have been morally neutral? If we defended ourself in court on the basis of the circumstances — that it was either break the speeding laws or permit our loved one to die — is there anyone who thinks that such evidence should really be excluded by the court in making its determination?

But how is this heroic effort that was made to save a human life in this situation any different from the illegal rescue missions at abortion clinics? If we sense any difference, is it only because in one case we can see the injured there before us, while in the other case the injured is hidden in the womb?

When there is a law against speeding or a law against trespassing, it cannot be pitted against a human life. It is a question of which is the greater evil and which is the lesser evil. It is not merely an issue of law, it is the predicament of the one being slaughtered. We recognize that questions such as, "When is civil disobedience justified?" "Why is it justified?" "To what extent is it justified?" and "How long should we wait before it is exercised?" are troubling. Violence is certainly out of the question, but Scripture does appear to support peaceful resistance to clearly social evil. (See Acts 5:29; Daniel 3:8–18; 6:16; Esther 3:2–6)

Argument against:

It is easy to understand the frustration of those in the Operation Rescue movement who feel that breaking the law is their only option. But there are better ways. More lives have probably been saved by the law-abiding methods we have just discussed than by breaking the law.

The Biblical arguments cited are not valid. There is no law in this country (as in China) forcing women to have an abortion. The scriptural illustrations given involve an attempt to force evil behavior. But women today are not ordered to have abortions. If we lived in China, the situation would be different. But even in ancient Rome, where the government permitted great evil, Paul did not tell Christians to oppose the law in order to restrict such evil but to submit to the authorities (see Romans 13: 1–6 and Esther 3–9).

It is incorrect to say that we must choose either to break the law or to kill children. No one is responsible for the deaths of unborn children except those directly involved. The current abortion laws are the problem, and the laws must be changed.

But in order to change one law, we are not scripturally authorized to break another.

Operation Rescue's method causes society to view pro-lifers as lawbreakers and produces unnecessary antagonism toward the pro-life cause. Anyone who considers these methods must carefully weigh the consequences of not only breaking the law (such as jail sentences and diminished capacity to work for legal reform) but of being perceived primarily as a lawbreaker.

The majority of Americans favor restricting abortion. The major problem which has brought about methods such as those in Operation Rescue is that too many people have done nothing at all to help change abortion laws. Therefore, some people feel that this has become the last desperate option to prevent abortions. The solution to the problem is for people to be more involved in changing the law.

Whatever our position, Scripture teaches we are not to be divided over how others choose to exercise their conscience before God (see Romans 14:4–12).

Questions for Discussion

1. Do you agree that even a single individual can have a great impact on social events?

2. Read 1 Timothy 2:1–2. Do you really feel that Christians should pray for those in authority that they will have wisdom from God? Ask yourself if you are spending enough time in prayer for our rulers.

3. Discuss with other Christian friends the ways in which you feel God would lead you or your church to be involved in stopping the legalization of abortion.

CONCLUSION

W e understand that reading this book may have been difficult. But we again want to encourage women who have been victims of abortion that substantial healing is possible.

One book in particular we recommend on this subject is *Help for the Post-Abortion Woman* (Zondervan, 1989) by Teri Reisser and Paul Reisser, M.D. Both authors have dealt extensively with the post-abortion syndrome. Again this book helps women to compassionately understand and resolve the aftermath of their abortion.

Personal counseling is also helpful, and such services are offered without cost by many groups, churches and organizations.

Finally, at some point, women may wish to help other women deal with this issue. It has been our experience that personally turning a negative situation into a positive one can be both an encouraging and healing experience.

Actually, some women who have had abortions have gone on to become some of the strongest pro-life advocates in the country (e.g., 9:xi-xxvi).

In terms of political activists, far more women are working against abortion than for it. For example, the National Right to Life Committee has 7.5 million women working to stop abortion and to provide positive alternatives. But even in the National Abortion Rights Action League and the National Organization of Women, there are less than 500,000 female members. In fact, for every one woman working for abortion, over 20 women are working against abortion (9:312-313).

Consider the story of Carol Everett (81:9-11). Carol knows about the trauma of abortion firsthand. Her own abortion precipitated an emotional crisis that resulted in a very painful divorce. She became the director of two successful Dallas area abortion clinics from 1977 to 1983. But she became consumed by guilt over the ever-present evidence that abortions were killing human children. She was also troubled by the considerable malpractice occurring at the expense of women who had been told abortion carried little or no risk.

Eventually Carol sold her very profitable business, contributing most of the proceeds to the Right to Life movement. She continues to support this movement through a heavy speaking schedule.

Carol's story is not unique. An increasing number of professionals are deserting the abortion industry. In fact, it has been their very experience in this industry that has catapulted them into the pro-life movement.

Perhaps a positive outlet for your own experience with abortion is to become involved in helping to support the Right to Life movement. As we stated at the beginning of this book, the best approach is to forget the past and press onward.

We must never underestimate the power of a single individual to contribute substantial change. Consumer advocate Ralph Nader is a good illustration of what one person can do. Looking back on his own highly successful career, he offers this wisdom: "The only way is to go forward. Learn from the past. Go forward. Never get discouraged."

We cannot but echo those words. Do not be discouraged. Go forward.

APPENDIX

THE SUPREME COURT
AND ABORTION

I n describing Governor Mario Cuomo's response to Bishop Vaughan's position on abortion, John Elson said:

> A fairer statement would be that the governor did not see how he could legally deny a woman what the nation's highest court has decreed to be her right. Second, the bishops have acted as if it were universally accepted that human life from the moment of conception is a person requiring legal protection. But that is a moral judgment, not scientific fact, disputed even by religious leaders who no more favor murder than do Catholic bishops. (*Time* [February 15, 1990]:75)

The Supreme Court and Abortion

The importance of the Supreme Court's *Roe v. Wade* decision in 1973 cannot be underestimated. "It is the first and crucial issue that has been overwhelming in changing attitudes toward the value of life in general" (16:34).

Why is it important for us to understand what the Supreme Court decided concerning abortion, and what was the basis for their decision? It is important for this reason: When the American public realizes the extent of bias and error behind that decision, their ruling will no longer command respect. It will be understood for what it was: unfounded social engineering. (See 101:301–328)

What Did the Supreme Court Decide?

The Supreme Court decided that at no point during the nine months of gestation is the unborn child protected by law:

> The court claimed the onset of a human being's life is presently unknowable. It denied the humanity of the unborn and assigned to them instead the pseudo-scientific status of "potential life." The justices defined abortion euphemistically as "termination of pregnancy." The fact that human life is destroyed was obscured. The notion that fundamental justice requires the protection of the innocent was never entertained. (8:26)

As Justice Rehnquist observed in his dissenting opinion, "a State may impose virtually no restriction on the performance of abortions." (99:196; 410 US 113 at 171)

In essence, *Roe v. Wade* and *Doe v. Bolton* (the 1973 companion case), in a wholly arbitrary manner, split pregnancy into three trimesters and issued rulings on each trimester. This resulted in overturning laws prohibiting abortion in virtually every state.

The Dissenting Opinions
in the *Roe v. Wade* Case

Seven justices agreed with the majority opinion written by Justice Harry Blackmun. The two dissenting justices — Byron White and William Rehnquist — forcefully stated that the majority opinion was wrong, noting that the Court had decreed — unconstitutionally — that any and all pregnancies can be terminated for any reason or for "no reason at all" even though they present "no danger whatever to the life or health of the mother but are nevertheless, unwanted for any one or more of a variety of reasons — convenience, family planning, economics, dislike of children, the embarrassment of illegitimacy, etc" (99:195; 410 US 113 at 221).

Further, Justices White and Rehnquist concluded they could "find nothing in the language or history of the Constitution to support the Court's judgment. The Court simply fashions and announces a new constitutional right for pregnant mothers and with scarcely any reason or authority for its action" (99:195; 410 US 113 at 221–222). The justices termed the decision "an improvident [careless and wasteful] and extravagant exercise of the power" granted to them by the Constitution, an unfortunate use of "raw judicial power" (99:196; 410 US 113 at 222).

Another dissenting opinion was provided by Congress itself. In 1981, the U.S. Senate Judiciary Subcommittee on Separation of Powers conducted extensive hearings on abortion in view of the Fourteenth Amendment's protection of human life. Some twenty-two physicians, scientists, and legal scholars testified, and the Subcommittee concluded that the question of when the life of a human being begins was already "answered by scientific, factual evidence" and that the major issue before them was the value of human life. "Pro-abortionists, though invited to do so, failed to produce a single expert witness who would specifically testify that life begins at any point other than conception or implantation" (85:3, 11–12; 100:113). What is important for our discussion here is that the Subcommittee concluded, ". . . now, basing our decision not upon science but upon the values embodied in our Constitution, we affirm the sanctity of all human life" (85:18).

Even Congress could see through the fallacies of the Supreme Court decision.

Some Reasons
Behind the Supreme Court Decision

All biologists then and now admit human life begins at conception. No one argues that it is morally right to kill innocent human life. How then did the Supreme Court come to such a decision? There are several reasons.

View of Life

The Supreme Court appealed to a pagan view of life over against a Christian view. It even noted that the ancient pagan attitudes they cited "are not capable of precise determination" but used them anyway in defense of its position (99:164; 410 US 113 at 130).

For example, Blackmun argued that "Greek and Roman law afforded little protection to the unborn," that abortion "was resorted to without scruple" and that, "ancient religion did not bar abortion" (99:164; 410 US 113 at 130). But Greek and Roman law not only permitted abortion but infanticide as well. Would the Supreme Court rule in favor of infanticide today, simply because it was an ancient practice? Further, now that abortion is legalized, could this mean it will not be long before the killing of infants really is legalized?

Viability

The Supreme Court argued that the state has no compelling interest in restricting abortion until the point of viability (i.e. that point at which the fetus can survive outside of the womb). The Court wrongly placed viability at six to seven months (410 US 113 at 160). Actually the Court not only incorrectly cited its own documentation (*Williams Obstetrics*, 14th edition, page 493; 410 US 113 at 160 ref. 60), but also it failed to note that even then twenty to thirty percent of infants were viable at four and a half months or twenty weeks (101:315). But the Court held that until six to seven months, allegedly, a human being is not "viable" or "capable of meaningful life" and therefore the state has no vested interested justifying its restriction of a women's choice to abortion (99:183; 410 US 113 at 163).

The problem with viability is that it is too slippery and unreliable a concept. The fetus is viable at all stages of pregnancy if it is left in its normal environment in the womb. Only when the fetus is removed from its natural environment does viability become an issue. In the next decade viability may be placed at ten to fifteen weeks. If an artificial placenta is developed, it will be placed at conception. The concept of viability is meaningless.

If viability is defined as the ability to survive outside the womb, and if dependence on some external "support system" is believed to render an individual "non-viable," then we must also define everyone with pacemakers, those who depend on kidney dialysis, and even insulin-dependent diabetics as "non-viable."

Bernard Nathanson, M.D., a former leader in the abortion industry who is now pro-life, has stated, "we have no tests [to determine] viability. Viability is a pathetically unreliable criterion for protection of a human being-under the law; there are so many variables and it is so poorly defined that it is all but useless" (51:3).

Only a Potential Person

The Supreme Court argued the unborn child was not a person with the right to equal protection under the law, but only a potential person.

The Court's view was that "the fetus, *at most,* represents *only* the potentiality of life" (99:182, emphasis added; 410 US 113 at 162). The problem here is that if we first assume life is not present (but only potential), then true life is not being destroyed in an abortion (410 US 113 at 218).

But the Court's assumption was wrong. (It even admitted that if it were wrong *here,* its entire decision "collapses for the fetus' right to life is then guaranteed specifically by the [Fourteenth] Amendment" (99:179; 410 US 113 at 156–157).) The zygote-fetus is not a "potential person" because:

- it is alive (not potentially alive)

- it has a unique human nature (not a potential human nature)

- at any stage of development it is most accurately described as an actual person with great potential

From zygote on, genetically and physically, a unique individual exists. It is an established scientific fact that full human life is present at conception (see question 6). Consider what Landrum B. Shettles, M.D., Ph.D., one of the world's leading scientists (100:9–15), states concerning a person's chromosomal heredity, one's "genotype":

> The power of genotype can scarcely be overestimated. Your genetic makeup—established the moment fertilization is completed and conception occurs—determines not only your physical characteristics, but also—more powerfully than anything else that can be demonstrated—how you will process information, how you will think, what you will be in what we call "mind." . . . The genotype that is conferred at conception does not merely start life, it *defines* life. (100:36–37)

The Supreme Court had access to all this data, but ignored it (85/95; 100:100–101; 99:181). Instead of giving a blanket promotion of abortion, why did they not, at the least, warn women that they could very well be taking human life—with all that implies in fact and consequence?

Refusal to Fairly Examine the Scientific Evidence

The Court refused to fairly examine the issue of when human life begins. The Court claimed, "we need not resolve the difficult question of when life begins. When those trained in the respective disciplines of medicine, philosophy, and theology are unable to arrive at any consensus, the judiciary, at this point in the development of man's knowledge, is not in a position to speculate as to the answer" (99:181; 410 US 113 at 159).

Of course, the issue of when human life begins never was an issue of philosophy or theology—only of science and medicine. The Court has traditionally accepted scientific facts over philosophical (and certainly theological) speculation—except in this case (100:110). Nor was the issue medically ever as uncertain or questionable as the Court implied it was (100:113; 101:318).

Contrary to the Court's claim, scientific consensus *did* exist that human life begins at conception, but again, the Court simply chose to ignore it. Medical experts had *already* unanimously testified before the Court that *human life begins at conception*. Why then did the Court not listen to them? (85; 100:110–111; 101:318; 99:179; 410 US 113 at 156).

On the John Ankerberg Show for March 4, 1990, Judie Brown, President of the American Life League, revealed the unknown background of *Roe v. Wade:*

> We've done a study of how *Roe v. Wade* came to pass because after Justice William O. Douglas passed away, all of his records were made available to the public. That was just one year ago. And we had a team of researchers go down and literally sort through 4,000 boxes of Justice Douglas' papers. And what we learned by studying all of those papers which related to the *Roe v. Wade* decision was really, really horrifying.

> First of all, we realized that Justice Brennan literally advised Justice Blackmun every step of the way on how to craft judicial arguments that would make it possible to legalize the killing of innocent babies. There is also a memo that Justice Blackmun sent to Justice Douglas in which he pointed out that his aim through *Roe v. Wade* was going to be to legalize abortion no matter what steps he had to take. He wanted to minimize the damage to the judicial process however, in such a way that he would come up with the most logical argument that the justices could possibly use that they had to legalize abortion.

> And so they knew when they took the case—*Roe v. Wade* and *Doe v. Bolton*—that they were in fact going to legalize abortion, the only question that was in their minds was how to do it. This is why the justices chose in 1972, when they heard the [scientific] arguments

[that life begins at conception], to eliminate all medical discussion from the hearing. There were no pieces of evidence allowed in that court room with regard to the humanity of the child in the womb. And that, in fact, was why the justices were able to say "physicians and theologians do not agree on when life begins so we will simply not discuss that issue. This is strictly an issue of a woman and her right to make a decision with her doctor."

So the humanity of the child was discounted immediately because Justice Blackmun and Justice Brennan both realized that if they were to take a good look at the evidence, medical evidence, with regard to the existence of the child, they would not be able to legalize abortion and they had already made up their minds they would legalize abortion.

Further, the Court wrongly held that conception could be *a process* rather than an event (99:181; 410 US 113 at 161). But this idea is totally false because scientists confess that "there is nothing in the whole of human development that deserves more to be called an event than does fertilization, nor is there anything else that involves such an essential change" (5:30). The bias of the Court should be evident. It *ignored* known scientific data — data presented before it and with which it was familiar — in order to "support" its ruling.

Right to Privacy

The Court's decision was based upon an alleged "right to privacy" supporting the right to an abortion. The Court asserted that women have a right to abortion which is derived from a broader constitutional right to privacy which the Court has historically recognized in the First, Fourth, Fifth, Ninth, and Fourteenth Amendments. But Blackmun himself confessed, "the Constitution does not explicitly mention any right of privacy" (99:176; 410 US 113 at 152, 153).

But even if there were an explicit Constitutional right to privacy, why should this have anything to do with abortion? If abortion is wrong because it is scientifically established that it is the killing of innocent human life, the alleged right to privacy is irrelevant. Abortions are wrong because they destroy human life. Somehow the Court decided this was not true.

The decision of the Supreme Court legalizing abortion was not only incorrect scientifically, legally, and morally, it was argued on extremely poor grounds in general. It is without doubt one of the worst examples of judicial activism in this century.

The Supreme Court alleged in the *Roe v. Wade* decision it had acted in society's best interest. But history has shown this was not the result.

The Unexpected Results of the Supreme Court Decision

The Court itself rejected "any claim that the Constitution requires abortion on demand" as well as the idea that a woman's right to an abortion is absolute (99:185, 177; 410 US 113 at 208, 153–154). Yet, these were the unexpected results. Today, abortion is a socially accepted form of birth control, and there were other unexpected results as well:

Result One

The killing of 26 million. How unprecedented this Court's power has been can only be understood in terms of the 26 million abortions since 1973. This is the equivalent of wiping out from existence the total populations of a half dozen smaller countries. That seven individuals wield this kind of power is frightening.

Result Two

Placing millions of women in varying degrees of jeopardy. Women are subject to serious physical and psychological consequences from an abortion. Francis Schaeffer and former U.S. Surgeon General C. Everett Koop observe, "abortion counselors rarely talk about physical dangers, emotional results, and psychological consequences. They seldom tell the woman what is going to happen or what may be involved" (16:52). Is this fair? Is this upholding the "rights" of women? (33:56).

Result Three

The moral compromising of the medical profession. The Supreme Court, in effect, has denied the mandate of the medical profession to uphold the sanctity of life. In the words of lawyer Mark Belz:

When the doctor performs an abortion, his act is equivalent to murder. . . . Consider once again the definition of murder: purposely or *knowingly*, without justification, causing the death of another human being. If language has meaning, abortion is murder. But *Roe v. Wade* has made it legal. The entire machinery of the system of jurisprudence in America, since January 22, 1973, has been engaged to promote, protect, and preserve the carrying out of this right to kill. (3:23–24 emhpasis added; see 98)

Result Four

The Supreme Court elevated abortion to a constitutional "right," thereby making all laws against abortion unconstitutional. Once the Supreme Court declared abortion a constitutional right, law prohibiting abortion became impossible. Thus, "the conclusion of the Court had the effect of overturning every law in the United States that attempted to prohibit abortion" (8:16–18).

Result Five

The Supreme Court decision potentially turned any mother against any given number of her children. Essentially, the Court assumed that whenever a conflict of "interests" exists between a mother and her future child that they exist as adversaries and that the mother has the right to dispose of the child's life should she desire. "Only when the child is not perceived as a threat to the mother does society provide him with protection and rights" (8:18, cf. 13:10). Neither the husband, boyfriend, nor parents may interfere with this decision in spite of their own rights concerning the child.

The Irrationality of the Court's Decision

Animal Rights

Animals are now guaranteed more legal rights and protections than unborn children. Everything from lousewort plants, orange-bellied mice and daddy-long-legs spiders have been legally protected, at great economic cost. Porpoises, whales, baby seals, and hundreds of other animals are all protected by law. But baby children are not. The very same Supreme Court which made possible the slaughter of tens of millions of unborn human babies stopped the construction of the

$116,000,000 Tellico Dam in Tennessee merely because it might cause a three-inch fish known as the "snail darter" to become extinct! (16:210).

Today we have laws regulating even the killing of stray dogs and cats; we have laws protecting all sorts of wild animals, from tiny fish to great whales; we have laws preventing acts of violence or cruelty to both animals and men; but we have no such laws preventing violence, cruelty, and killing being exercised toward unborn human beings. We can do horrible things to the pre-born that we are legally prohibited from doing to dogs or even hamsters!

Child Abuse

Child abuse became legal — as long as the child was still in the womb. Those parents who abuse or beat their infant children are taken to jail for their crimes. But those parents who help abuse and destroy their infants in the womb are well within their legal rights. Can we logically maintain that it is morally wrong to beat a three-month-old infant to death merely because he is outside the womb while we accept the murder of a six-month-old pre-born infant merely because he is still in the womb?

Right to Live Denied

The other legal rights of the unborn were maintained; only their right to live was denied. In property and inheritance law, anglo-american jurisprudence has scrupulously maintained the rights of the unborn, accepting that human life begins at conception (35:53, cf. pp. 43, 58–59). All of us are familiar with "wrongful death" lawsuits against persons who accidentally injure unborn children to the point of their death. "To this day, the law recognizes unborn children as persons entitled to all these rights. In fact, criminals who have assaulted pregnant women have been successfully prosecuted for murder when the unborn child has been killed. Nevertheless, the law regards the unborn as a non-person when a mother is willing to destroy him" (8:18, cf. 35:25–75).

Doctors

Doctors were charged to both save life and to destroy it. All laws attempting to prohibit abortion after viability have been declared unconstitutional. But the Supreme Court does allow "that two doctors be present when viable infants are aborted—one to kill the baby through abortion and one to care for the infant should the first doctor fail" (8:31). Further, if during an abortion procedure the child is killed while in the womb, no law is broken, but if that same child is removed from the womb and killed outside the woman, the physician is liable to a charge of murder.

Where Do We Stand
After Webster and Subsequent Cases?

On July 3, 1989, the Supreme Court announced its decision in *Webster v. Reproductive Health Services* relating to the state of Missouri. Perhaps the most significant event in *Webster* is that for the first time in sixteen years the Court refused a request to expand abortion rights. It must be remembered that the Supreme Court did not strike down Missouri law which requires doctors to perform various tests to determine the viability of a baby at twenty weeks prior to an abortion. But neither did it extend Missouri law to other states. Further, the Court did not overrule the central tenet of *Roe*—the right to abortion on demand given by an unwritten constitutional right of privacy. The Court "technically avoided modifying any part of the counter-regulatory scheme elaborated during the last sixteen years by *Roe* and its progeny" (70:34).

The *Webster* decision continues to underscore the schizophrenic nature of the Court. It retained *Roe* but let stand the preamble of the Missouri law asserting that the life of every human being begins at conception and that the interests of the unborn may be protected in areas of life, health, and well-being.

What can be done? Until now, legislators have been able to hide behind *Roe v. Wade.* Their problem is one of political perception and having to face "pro-choice" intimidation and propaganda. Their problem is *not* scientific facts concerning the unborn.

Unfortunately, events to date indicate many politicians are more concerned about their own political lives rather than the lives of the unborn. Because unrestricted abortion was the law of the land, they could argue that any attempt to legislate changes would only be struck down by federal courts. The value of *Webster* is that this situation no longer exists. Dr. Nathanson suggests we supply these legislators with sufficient scientific information to resist the political intimidation of the pro-choice camp (51:1).

Conclusion

Until abortion is decided on strictly factual, scientific, and moral grounds, abortion will continue to be bandied about state by state. What is needed is a federal statute to protect the unborn from the moment of conception in all fifty states. Their rights as persons under the Fifth and Fourteenth Amendments need to be guaranteed by a constitutional amendment. Otherwise, the state legislatures, the media, and the powerful pro-choice propaganda interests may continue to overrule the wishes of the majority of Americans.

Constitutional interpretations can be overruled in two ways:

- by a constitutional amendment—a very difficult process

- by judicial willingness to reevaluate "judge-made law" (70:35)

The problem with the latter is that judges can revise their opinions again and again depending on a variety of social or other circumstances. The constitutional amendment, while much more difficult to implement, is the only option commensurate to the importance of the issue involved in protecting human beings in the womb once and for all.

BIBLIOGRAPHY

(Note: References in the text are keyed to the bibliography and cited by title and page. References to the 1973 Supreme Court *Roe v. Wade* decision are taken from U.S. Supreme Court Reports, Vol. 35 (1973) (ref. 99) and cite case data. For easier reading some lengthy paragraph quotations have been subparagraphed. If a secondary source is cited, the reader should assume it contains the primary reference. Key to markings: *Recommended reading. **Essential reading)

*1.   James K. Hoffmeier (ed.), *Abortion: A Christian Understanding and Response,* Grand Rapids, MI: Baker, 1987.

*2.   Jean S. Garton, *Who Broke the Baby,* Minneapolis, MN: Bethany, 1979. (Order from Life Cycle Books, 2205 Danforth Avenue, Toronto, Ontario M4C 1K4.)

*3.   Mark Belz, *Suffer the Little Children: Christians, Abortion and Civil Disobedience,* Westchester, IL: Crossway Books, 1989.

4.   John Warwick Montgomery, *Slaughter of the Innocents: Abortion, Birth Control and Divorce in Light of Science, Law and Theology,* Westchester, IL: Cornerstone Books, 1981.

*5.   Ronald Reagan, *Abortion and the Conscience of the Nation,* Nashville, TN: Thomas Nelson, 1984.

6.   Harold O. J. Brown, *Death Before Birth,* Nashville, TN: Thomas Nelson, 1977.

*7.   Paul Fowler, *Abortion: Toward an Evangelical Consensus,* Portland, OR: Multnomah Press, 1987.

*8.   Curt Young, *The Least of These: What Everyone Should Know About Abortion,* Chicago, IL: Moody Press, 1984.

**9.   David Reardon, *Aborted Women: Silent No More*, Westchester, IL: Crossway, 1987.

*10.   Daniel Callahan, *Abortion: Law, Choice and Morality*, New York: Macmillan, 1972.

*11.   Thomas W. Hilgers, M.D., Dennis J. Horan and David Mall (eds.), *New Perspectives on Human Abortion*, Frederick, MD: University Publications of America, Inc./Aletheia Books, 1981.

12.   John Stott, *Involvement: Social and Sexual Relationships in the Modern World Volume 2*, Old Tappan, NJ: Fleming Revelle, 1985.

**13.   John T. Noonan, Jr., *A Private Choice: Abortion in America in the 70s*, New York: The Free Press/Macmillan, 1979.

14.   John T. Noonan, Jr. (ed.), *The Morality of Abortion: Legal and Historical Perspectives*, Cambridge, MA: Harvard University Press, 1972.

15.   Walter O. Spitzer and Carlyle L. Saylor (eds.), *Birth Control and the Christian: A Protestant Symposium on the Control of Human Reproduction*, Wheaton, IL: Tyndale, 1969.

16.   Francis A. Schaeffer, C. Everett Koop, M.D., *Whatever Happened to the Human Race?*, Old Tappan, NJ: Fleming H. Revelle, 1979.

17.   "Exclusive Interview: U.S. Surgeon General C. Everett Koop," *Rutherford Journal*, Manassas, VA, The Rutherford Institute, Spring 1989, pp. 30-37.

18.   John Ankerberg, "Is Abortion a Justifiable Practice?," unpublished paper.

19.   John Ankerberg, "Creationist vs. Traducianist Views," unpublished paper.

20.   John Jefferson Davis, "Abortion," (Chapter 6), *Evangelical Ethics*, Phillipsburg, NJ: Presbyterian and Reformed, 1985.

21.   *Christianity Today*, July 14, 1989.

22.   *Christianity Today*, August 18, 1989.

23.   "Is Abortion Justifiable?," *News and Views*, May 1988, Chattanooga, TN, The John Ankerberg Evangelistic Association.

24.   Landrum B. Shettles and David Rorvik, "Human Life Begins at Conception," in *Abortion: Opposing Viewpoints*, New York: Greenhaven Press, 1986.

25. Dr. and Mrs. J. C. Willke, *Handbook on Abortion and Abortion Questions and Answers,* Hayes Publishing Co., 1985.

26. R. F. R. Gardner, *Abortion: The Personal Dilemma,* Old Tappan, NJ: William B. Eerdmans, 1972.

27. Robert E. and Mary R. Joyce, *Let Us Be Born,* Franciscan Herald Press, 1970.

*28. Clifford E. Bajema, *Abortion and the Meaning of Personhood,* Grand Rapids, MI: Baker, 1974. A summary of the brief can be found in John M. Langone, "Abortion: The Medical Evidence Against," *The Cambridge Fish,* Vol. 2, no. 1.

29. Robert J. Ohrstedt, "Abortion: Focus of Conflict," *Currents in Theology and Mission,* June 1986.

*30. Steven C. Meyer, "Fully Formed: The Discoveries of Fetology," *Eternity,* June 1985.

31. *Time,* October 10, 1988, p. 103; *Newsweek,* December 29, 1986, p. 47; *Time,* November 7, 1988, p. 103; *Christianity Today,* October 7, 1983, pp. 71-72; *Christianity Today,* July 11, 1986, p. 37; *U.S. News and World Report,* January 23, 1989, p. 54; *Scientific American,* December 1986, pp. 81-82.

*32. Patrick Dixon, *The Whole Truth About AIDS,* Nashville, TN: Thomas Nelson, 1989.

*33. Debra Evans, *Without Moral Limits: Women, Reproduction and the New Medical Technology,* Westchester, IL: Crossway Books, 1989.

*34. Herbert T. Krimmel and Martin J. Foley, "Abortion and Human Life: A Christian Perspective," *The Simon Greenleaf Law Review,* Vol. 5 (1985-1986), Anaheim, CA, The Simon Greenleaf School of Law.

35. John Warwick Montgomery, "The Rights of the Unborn Children," *The Simon Greenleaf Law Review,* Vol. 5 (1985-1986), Anaheim, CA, The Simon Greenleaf School of Law.

36. Meredith G. Kline, "Lex Talionis and the Human Fetus," *The Simon Greenleaf Law Review,* Vol. 5 (1985-1986), Anaheim, CA, The Simon Greenleaf School of Law.

37. David K. Clark, "An Evaluation of the Quality of Life Argument for Infanticide," *The Simon Greenleaf Law Review,* Vol. 5 (1985-1986), Anaheim, CA, The Simon Greenleaf School of Law.

38. Allan Spragget and Ross Peterson: *The New Edgar Cayce,* New York: Doubleday, 1977.

39. Cynthia Bohannon, *The North and South Nodes: The Guidepost of the Spirit: A Comprehensive Interpretation of the Nodal Placements,* Jacksonville, FL: Arthur Publications, 1987.

*40. Joseph M. Scheider, *Closed: 99 Ways to Stop Abortion,* Westchester, IL: Crossway Books, 1985.

*41. John Warwick Montgomery, "Editors Introduction," *The Simon Greenleaf Law Review,* Vol. 5 (1985-1986), Anaheim, CA, The Simon Greenleaf School of Law.

**42. Vincent M. Rue, et.al., *A Report on the Psychological Aftermath of Abortion* (presented to C. Everett Koop by the National Right to Life Committee) September 15, 1987, Washington, D.C.: National Right to Life Committee, 1987. Appendix One summarizes 90 studies.

*43. Richard Glasow, "Planned Parenthood: The Nation's Leading Provider and Promoter of Abortion" brochure, September, 1988, Washington, D.C., National Right to Life Committee.

44. Melody Green, "The Questions Most People Ask About Abortion," *Last Days Magazine* (Box 70, Lyndale, TX 75771-0070 RPT, n.d.).

45. P. Ney, "A Consideration of Abortion Survivors," *Child Psychiatry and Human Development,* Vol. 13, 1982, pp. 168-79.

46. Bernard N. Nathanson, "Deeper into Abortion," *New England Journal of Medicine,* November 28, 1974.

47. The National Right to Life Educational Trust Fund, "Abortion: The Hard Cases," Tract, Washington, D.C., NRLETF, 1987.

48. John Powell, *Abortion: The Silent Holocaust,* Allen, TX: Argus, 1981.

49. The National Right to Life Educational Trust Fund, "Abortion: Public Opinion," Tract, Washington, D.C., NRLETF, 1987, citing e.g., *Public Opinion Quarterly,* Vol. 45 (1981), pp. 216-23 and Edward Manier (ed.), *Abortion: New Directions for Policy Studies,* 1977, pp. 51-82.

*50. Gary Bergel and C. Everett Koop, *When You Were Formed in Secret,* Reston, VA: Intercessors for America, P.O. Box 2639, Reston, VA 22090 (703-471-0913).

*51. Bernard N. Nathanson, M.D. (technical ed.), *Bernadell Technical Bulletin,* October 1989, Vol. 1, No. 1, Bernadell, Inc., P.O. Box

1897, New York, NY 10011. Articles on Webster, viability, abortifacients, etc.

52. Irvin M. Cushner, M.D., U.S. Congress, Senate Committee on the Judiciary, *Constitutional Amendments Relating to Abortion,* S.J. res. 17, S.J., res. 18, S.J. Res. 19, and S.J. Res. 110, Ninety-seventh Congress, First Session, 1983, Vol. 1, p. 158.

53. B. Peterson, F. Barbash, and C. Russel, "After *Roe v. Wade:* Ten Years Conflict Over Abortion," *The Washington Post,* January 23, 1983.

*54. Bernard Nathanson, M.D., with Richard Ostling, *Aborting America,* Garden City, NY: Doubleday, 1979.

55. R. Furlong and R. Black, "Pregnancy Termination for Genetic Indications: The Impact of Families," *Social Work Health Care,* Vol. 10, (1984), pp. 17-34.

56. Interview with Coleman McCarthy, "Does Abortion Harden Maternal Instinct?," *National Catholic Reporter,* February 24, 1989.

57. American Rights Coalition, *The Abortion Injury Report,* September 1989, p. 2, Chattanooga, TN, American Rights Coalition (1-800-634-2224).

*58. Wanda Franz, Testimony, U.S. Congress, House, Human Resources and Intergovernmental Relations Subcommittee of the Committee on Government Operations, Hearing on *Medical and Psychological Impact of Abortion,* 101st cong., first session, March 16, 1989. See also Vincent Rue, *The Hatch Hearings,* Vol. 1, pp. 329-378; N. Spreckhard, *The Psycho-Social Stress Following Abortion,* Kansas City, MO: Sheed and Ward, 1987; N. Spreckhard (ed.), *Post Abortion Trauma* (1987); David Mall and Walter F. Watts, M.D. (ed.), *Psychological Aspects of Abortion,* Frederick, MD: University Publications of American 1979.

59. Carol Everett, "What I Saw in the Abortion Industry," Jefferson City, MO: Easton Publishing, 1988.

60. National Right to Life Educational Trust Fund, "Abortion: Some Medical Facts," Washington, D.C., NRLETF, 1989.

61. Faye Wattleton and Marcia Ann Gillespie, "Reprowoman," *Ms.,* October, 1989.

*62. George Grant, *Grand Illusions,* Brentwood, TN: Wolgemuth and Hyatt, 1988.

63. See e.g., Jean Michael Angebert, *The Occult and the Third Reich;* Gerald Suster, *Hitler: The Occult Messiah;* On Manson e.g., Arthur Lyons, *Satan Wants You,* New York: Mysterious Press, 1988, pp. 88-89.

64. Csaba Vedlik, "The Federal Situation Post Webster," (3 page report), Stafford, VA: American Life Lobby, Inc., 1989.

65. Linda Bird Franke, *The Ambivalence of Abortion,* New York: Random House, 1978 (personal experiences of abortion).

66. *Action* (monthly publication of the Rutherford Institute, Manassas, VA), October, 1989.

67. Richard A. McCormick, et al., "Abortion: What Does Webster Mean?," *Commonweal,* August 11, 1989.

68. Norman Geisler, *Ethics, Alternatives and Issues,* Grand Rapids, MI: Zondervan, 1971.

69. Norman Anderson, *Issues of Life and Death,* Downers Grove, IL: InterVarsity Press, 1977.

70. Grover J. Rees, "Scourge or Plot?," *National Review,* August 4, 1989.

71. Scientists for Life, Inc. and Edward C. Freiling, *The Position of Modern Science on the Beginning of Human Life,* Faxton, VA: Sun Life, 1983.

72. Norman L. Geisler, *Christian Ethics: Options and Issues,* Grand Rapids, MI: Baker, 1989.

73. Brian Young J.D., *Model State Laws,* Stafford, VA: American Life League, Inc., 1989.

74. Copy of House Bill HR624, January 24, 1989.

**75. Robert Evangelisto, *The Moral and Logical Arguments Against Abortion,* Stafford, VA: American Life League, Inc., n.d.

76. American Life League, Inc., *Black Genocide: The Facts,* Stafford, VA: American Life League, n.d.

*77. American Life League, "Who Was Margaret Sanger?," Stafford, VA: American Life League, n.d.

78. Robert G. Marshall, *Dissolving Compromise by the Study of Truth,* Stafford, VA: American Life League, Inc., n.d. c.f., "Dr. Koop's Non-report," p. 5, end pages.

*79.   Germain Grisez, *Abortion: The Myths, the Realities and the Arguments,* New York: Corpus Books, 1970.

80.   "Saturday Night with Connie Chung," November 18, 1989; initial transcript, p. 5.

*81.   Richard Exley, *Abortion: Pro-life by Conviction, Pro-choice by Default,* Tulsa, OK: Honor Books, 1989.

**82.   The Rutherford Institute, *Major Articles and Books Concerning the Detrimental Effects of Abortion* (Summary report from hundreds of scientific studies published in medical and psychological journals), Manassas, VA (P.O. Box 510), The Rutherford Institute.

83.   Robert G. Castadot, "Pregnancy Termination: Techniques, Risks and Complications and Their Management," *Fertility and Sterility,* Vol. 45, January 1986; Christopher Tietze, *Induced Abortion, a World Review,* New York: The Population Council, 1983, p. 83; Willard Cates and David A. Grimes, "Deaths From Second Trimester Abortion by Dilation and Evacuation: Causes, Prevention, Facilities," *Obstetrics and Gynecology,* Vol. 58, October 1981, pp. 401-408; Willard Cates, Richard M. Selick and Carl W. Tyler, "Behavioral Factors Contributing to Abortion Deaths: A New Approach to Mortality Studies," *Obstetrics and Gynecology,* Vol. 58, November 1981, p. 631; Christopher R. Harman, David G. Fish and John E. Tyson, "Factors Influencing Morbidity and Termination of Pregnancy," *American Journal of Obstetrics and Gynecology,* February 1, 1981, pp. 333-337.

84.   William D. Halsey (ed. director), *Macmillan Dictionary for Students,* New York: Macmillan, 1984.

85.   The Subcommittee on Separation of Powers, *Report to Senate Judiciary Committee Regarding the Human Life Bill,* S-158, 97th Congress, 1st Session, 1981.

86.   Erwin W. Lutzer, *Exploding the Myths That Could Destroy America,* Chicago, IL: Moody Press, 1986.

*87.   Initial transcript, The Ankerberg Theological Research Institute, "Is Abortion Justifiable?" televised program, Jan., 1990.

88.   See Stephen Hawking, *A Brief History of Time,* New York: Bantam, 1988.

89.   George Orwell, *1984,* New York: Signet, 1983.

90. G. L. Flanagan, *The First Nine Months of Life,* New York: Simon and Schuster, 1962.

91. M. Liley and B. Day, *Modern Motherhood,* New York: Random House, 1969.

*92. A. Ingleman-Sundberg and C. Wirsen, *A Child Is Born: The Drama of Life Before Birth,* New York: Delacorte Press, 1965.

93. Theodosius Dobzhansky, *Evolution, Genetics and Man,* Wiley and Sons, 1961.

94. Ashley Montagu, *Human Heredity,* World, 1963.

*95. Motion filed in the Supreme Court of the United States, October 15, 1971 (Re: No. 70-18 and No. 70-40). Titled "Motion and Brief Amicus Curiae of Certain Physicians, Professionals and Fellows of the American College of Obstetrics and Gynecology in Support of Appellees, Dennis J. Horan et al.," United States District Court 1971.

96. Douglas M. Considine (ed.), *Van Nostrand's Scientific Encyclopedia,* Sixth ed., New York: Van Nostrand Reinhold Co., 1983.

97. *California Medicine,* Vol. 113, no. 3 (Sept. 1970), pp. 67-68.

**98. William Brennan, *Medical Holocausts, Exterminative Medicine in Nazi Germany and Contemporary America,* Boston, MA: Nordland Pub. International, Inc., 1980, Vol. 1

**99. "Lawyer Cooperative," *U. S. Supreme Court Reports,* Vol. 35 (1974), *Roe v. Wade,* 410 US 113.

**100. Landrum B. Shettles, *Rites of Life: The Scientific Evidence for Life Before Birth,* Grand Rapids, MI: Zondervan, 1983.

**101. Thomas W. Hilgers and Dennis J. Horan, *Abortion and Social Justice,* Thaxton, VA: Sun Life, 1980.

102. Thomas A. Mappes and Jane S. Zemlaty, *Biomedical Ethics,* New York: McGraw Hill, 1986, 2nd ed.

103. Lynn D. Wordle, "Sanctioned Assisted Suicide: Separate But Equal Treatment for the New Illegitimates," *Issues in Law and Medicine,* Vol. 3, no. 3 (1987); Joseph Richman, "Sanctioned Assisted Suicide Impact on Family Relations," *Issues in Law and Medicine,* Vol. 3, no. 3 (1987). cf. Dennis J. Horan (ed.), *Infanticide and the Handicapped Newborn,* (1982); M. Kohl (ed.), *Infanticide and the Value of Life,* (1978).

104. Keith L. Moore, *The Developing Human: Clinically Oriented Embryology,* Philadelphia, PA: W.B. Sanders, 1982.

105. *Encyclopedia and Dictionary of Medicine Nursing and Allied Health,* Philadelphia: W.B. Sanders Co., 1978 2nd ed.

106. W. T. Reich (Ed. in chief), *Encyclopedia of Bioethics,* Georgetown University: The Free Press, 1978.

107. T. Richards, "Can a Fetus Feel Pain?," *British Medical Journal,* Nov. 2, 1985.

*108. Marjorie A. England, *Color Atlas of Life Before Birth: Normal Fetal Development,* Chicago, IL: Year Book Medical Pubs., Inc., 1983.

109. Claudia P. Mangel, "Legal Abortions: The Impending Obsolescence of the Trimester Framework," *American Journal of Law and Medicine,* Vol. 14, no. 1 (1988).

110. John Warwick Montgomery, *History and Christianity,* San Bernardino, CA: Here's Life, 1984; Norman L. Geisler and William E. Nix, *A General Introduction to the Bible,* Chicago: Moody Press, 1988 Rev.; Josh McDowell, *Evidence that Demands a Verdict,* Vol. 1 and 2; Ronald Nash, *Christian Faith and Historical Understanding,* Grand Rapids: Zondervan; F. F. Bruce, *The New Testament Documents: Are They Reliable?,* Downers Grove, IL: InterVarsity, 1973; R. Pache, *The Inspiration and Authority of Scripture,* Chicago: Moody Press, 1980; Gary Habermas, *The Verdict of History,* Nashville, TN: Thomas Nelson, 1988.

111. e.g., William Lane Craig, *The Son Rises,* Chicago: Moody Press, 1986; Frank Morison, *Who Moved the Stone?,* Downers Grove, IL: InterVarsity, 1965; Gary Habermas, *The Resurrection of Jesus,* Grand Rapids: Baker, 1980, cf. *The Simon Greenleaf Law Review,* Vol. 7 (1987-1988), Anaheim, CA: The Simon Greenleaf School of Law.

112. R. T. France, *Jesus and the Old Testament,* Grand Rapids, MI: Baker, 1982; John Wenham, *Christ and the Bible,* Downers Grove, IL: InterVarsity, 1973.

113. e.g., John Ankerberg, John Weldon, and Walter Kaiser, *The Case for Jesus the Messiah,* Eugene, OR: Harvest House, 1988.

114. L. Russ Bush (ed.), *Classical Readings in Christian Apologetics: AD 100-1800,* Grand Rapids: Zondervan, 1983.

115. J. N. D. Anderson, *Christianity and Comparative Religion,* Downers Grove, IL: InterVarsity, 1970; David L. Johnson, *A Personal Look at Asian Religions,* Minneapolis, MN: Bethany, 1985; Robert E. Speer, *The Finality of Jesus Christ,* Grand Rapids, MI: Zondervan, 1968.

116. Eusebius (ed./Tr. W. J. Ferrar), *The Proof of the Gospel,* Grand Rapids, MI: Baker, 1981 (rpt).

117. e.g., the Apostle Paul (Acts 9:1-2; 1 Cor. 15:3-8); Athanagoras (a second century scholar and first head of the school of Alexandria) who originally intended to write against Christianity (114:31); C. S. Lewis (See his *Surprised by Joy; Mere Christianity*); John Warwick Montgomery (See his *Faith Founded on Fact*); Sir William Ramsay, *The Bearing of Recent Discovery on the Trustworthiness of the New Testament,* Grand Rapids, MI: Baker, 1979; George Lyttleton and Gilbert West (see ref. 137); see also Josh McDowell, *Evidence That Demands a Verdict,* Vols. 1 and 2, San Bernardino, CA: Here's Life Publishers, 1980.

118. e.g., Geisler and Nix and Pache in 110

119. Lord Chancellor Hailsham, "The Door Wherein I Went," *The Simon Greenleaf Law Review,* Vol. 4, The Simon Greenleaf School of Law, Anaheim, CA; Hugo Grotius ("the father of international law"), *The Truth of Christian Religion* (1627); Harvard Law School Professor Simon Greenleaf (the greatest authority on English and Common-law evidence), *Testimony of the Evangelists* (rpt. in John Warwick Montgomery, *The Law Above the Law,* Minneapolis, MN: Bethany, 1985, app. 1, pp. 91-140); Edmund H. Bennett (for 20 years Dean of Boston University Law School), *The Four Gospels from a Lawyer's Standpoint* (1899); Irwin H. Linton, *A Lawyer Examines the Bible,* San Diego, CA: Creation Life, 1977, Santee, CA, Master Books; Judge Clarence Bartlett, *As a Lawyer Sees Jesus,* Cincinnati, Ohio: Standard, 1960; Lord Diploch (See *The Simon Greenleaf Law Review,* Vol. 5, pp. 213-216); Thomas Sherlock, *The Trial of the Witnesses of the Resurrection of Jesus* (rpt. in John Warwick Montgomery, *Jurisprudence: A Book of Readings,* (1974); Stephen D. Williams, *The Bible in Court: A Brief for the Plaintiff* (1925); J. N. D. Anderson, *Christianity: The Witness of History,* London: Tyndale, 1970; Frank Morrison, ref. 111, op. cit.

120. Umberto Cassuto, *Commentary on the Book of Exodus,* Jerusalem: Magnes Press, The Hebrew University, 1967.

121. Bruce K. Waltke, "Old Testament Texts Bearing on the Problem of the Control of Human Reproduction," in Walter O. Spitzer and Car-

lyle L. Sayor (eds.), *Birth Control and the Christian,* Wheaton, IL: Tyndale, 1969.

122. Television program transcript, "Abortion," Chattanooga, TN, The John Ankerberg Evangelistic Association, 1982.

123. C. F. Keil and F. Delitzsch, *Commentary on the Old Testament in Ten Volumes,* Vol. 1 (Exodus), Grand Rapids, MI: Eerdmans, 1978.

124. For sound critiques of evolutionary theory see R. L. Wysong, *The Creation-Evolution Controversy,* East Lansing, MI: Inquiry Press, 1985 and W. R. Bird, *The Origin of Species Revisited,* New York: Philosophical Library, 1989.

125. William M. Ramsay, *The Bearing of Recent Discovery on the Trustworthiness of the New Testament,* Grand Rapids, MI: Baker, 1979, rpt.

126. Pache and Geisler/Nix in 110; Ernst Wurthwein, *The Text of the Old Testament,* Grand Rapids, MI: Eerdmans, 1981.

127. "State Policies on Medicaid Funding of Abortion," National Right to Life Committee, Inc., October 24, 1989.

128. "AMA takes Pro-choice Policy Stand," *Chattanooga News Free Press,* December 6, 1989.

129. Ref. 103, in Horan (ed.).

*130. Randall A. Terry, *Operation Rescue,* Pittsburgh: Whitaker House, 1988.

131. Bob Frishman, *American Families: Responding to the Pro-family Movement,* Washington, D.C.: People for the American Way, 1984.

132. Jerry Falwell, *If I Should Die Before I Wake,* Nashville: Thomas Nelson, 1986.

133. S. Rickly Christian, *The Woodland Hills Tragedy: The Full Story Behind the 16,433 Aborted Babies Found in a California Suburb,* Westchester, IL: Crossway Books, 1985.

134. Leon R. Cass, M.D., Ph.D., "Prenatal Diagnosis and the Human Right to Life," *Studies in Law and Medicine,* No. 8, Chicago, IL: Americans United for Life, Inc., n.d.

135. James Burtchaell, "How Much Should a Child Cost?," *Studies in Law and Medicine,* No. 7, Chicago, IL: Americans United for Life, Inc., nd.

136. James M. Humber and Robert F. Almeder, *Biomedical Ethics and the Law,* New York: Plenum Press, 1976.

137. Letter from the Honourable George Lyttleton, Esq., Member of Parliament and the Commissioners of the Treasury to Gilbert West, MDCCLXI (1761), American Antiquities Society—A Reader Microprint. Early American Imprints No. 8909 (1631-1800AD). AC-4-E15 Box 22.

138. Michael Tooley, *Abortion and Infanticide,* Oxford: Clarendon Press, 1983.

139. John C. Fletcher and Mark I. Evans, "Maternal Bonding in Early Fetal Ultrasound Examinations," *New England Journal of Medicine,* February 17, 1983.

140. *Bernadell Technical Bulletin,* November 1989. (See ref. 21.)

*141. Dennis J. Horan et. al. (eds.), *Abortion and the Constitution,* Washington, DC: Georgetown University Press, 1987.

142. Jeffrey A. Aman and H. Wayne House, *Memphis State University Law Review,* Vol. 18, No. 1 (Fall 1987).

143. "Abortion: Hard Questions and Elusive Answers" *USA Today,* April 24. 1984.

144. Americans United For Life Legal Defense Fund, "On Pain Experienced by Fetuses in Abortions," Chicago, IL: AUFLDF, compiled data, nd. cf. *Chicago Sun Times* "26 Doctors Agree: Fetuses Feel Pain," February 14, 1984.

145. Paul de Parrie, *Rescuers,* Brentwood, TN: Wolgemuth & Hyatt, 1989.

ABOUT THE AUTHORS

John Ankerberg graduated from the University of Illinois with the B.A. degree, holds the Master of Divinity degree and a Master of Arts degree in Church History and the History of Christian Thought from Trinity Evangelical Divinity School in Deerfield, Illinois. He speaks internationally and is host of the nationally televised award-winning "The John Ankerberg Show." Over the last ten years he has hosted three separate televised debates on abortion. One of the series featured an American Civil Liberties Union attorney, a doctor performing abortions, a national pro-life advocate, and an attorney that helped prepare the brief presented before the Illinois Supreme Court arguing that unborn children in the womb should be protected.

John Weldon, M.Div., Ph.D., D.Min., M.A., has degrees in sociology, Biblical studies, comparative religion, and Christian apologetics. He is a graduate of California State University, San Diego; the Simon Greenleaf School of Law, Anaheim, California; Luther Rice Seminary, Jacksonville, Florida; William Carey International University, Pasadena, California; and Pacific College of Graduate Studies, Melbourne, Australia. He is currently Senior Researcher for "The John Ankerberg Show." He was once a supporter of women's rights to abortion.

Every Sunday night "The John Ankerberg Show" can be seen nationally on the CBN Cable Network at 10:30 Eastern time. It may be seen on other fine stations (check your local listing for time and day).

The typeface for the text of this book is *Times Roman*. In 1930, typographer Stanley Morison joined the staff of *The Times* (London) to supervise design of a typeface for the reformatting of this renowned English daily. Morison had overseen type-library reforms at Cambridge University Press in 1925, but this new task would prove a formidable challenge despite a decade of experience in paleography, calligraphy, and typography. *Times New Roman* was credited as coming from Morison's original pencil renderings in the first years of the 1930s, but the typeface went through numerous changes under the scrutiny of a critical committee of dissatisfied *Times* staffers and editors. The resulting typeface, *Times Roman*, has been called the most used, most successful typeface of this century. The design is of enduring value to English and American printers and publishers, who choose the typeface for its readability and economy when run on today's high-speed presses.

Cover Design:
Steve Diggs & Friends
Nashville, Tennessee

Page Composition:
Xerox Ventura Publisher
Printware 720 IQ Laser Printer

Printing and Binding:
Dickinson Press Inc.
Grand Rapids, Michigan